WORD WORK
WORD STUDY
TEACHER GUIDE

CONTRIBUTING AUTHOR

E. Judith Cohen, Ed.D.
College of Education
Department of Educational Psychology and Special Education
Florida International University
Miami, FL

CONSULTANTS

Catherine Bishop
Reading Resource Specialist
Greenfield Union School District
Bakersfield, CA

Susie Boutry
Intermediate Teacher
Narrows View Intermediate School
University Place School District
University Place, WA

Karen Eades McMullen
Reading Specialist
Tempe School District 3
Tempe, AZ

Lois Lanning, Ph.D.
Assistant Superintendent
of Schools
Pomperaug Regional
School District 15
Middlebury, CT

Glenda Nugent
Literacy Consultant
Little Rock, AR

Connie Ramsey
Whitworth College M.I.T.
Instructor
Learning Assistance
Program Teacher
Colbert Elementary
Mead School District
Mead, WA

Lillian Vega Castaneda, Ed.D.
Professor
California State University
Channel Islands
Camarillo, CA

Wright
Group

Fast Track Reading Word Study Teacher's Guide
©2002 Wright Group/McGraw-Hill

Wright Group/McGraw-Hill
19201 120th Avenue NE, Suite 100
Bothell, WA 98011
www.WrightGroup.com

Printed in the United States

10 9 8 7 6 5 4 3 2

ISBN: 0-322-06004-4

CONTENTS

The Research Behind Fast Track Reading Word Study

Normally achieving children add about 3000 words per year to their meaning vocabularies, yet teachers can reasonably teach the meanings of only between 300 and 400 words per year. (Nagy, Anderson, Herman 1987; Nagy 1988) From this it appears that students must learn the bulk of these 3000 words through contextual reading. Because poorer readers read much less text than good readers, and because the material they read contains considerably less difficult or new vocabulary, poorer readers will continue to fall behind. Stahl and Shiel (1999) suggest that "[e]ach word that is not understood, or partially or inflexibly understood, adds to the child's misunderstandings, leading the child further and further from the author's intended meaning." In order to support poorer readers, they need to be provided with an opportunity to learn how words are constructed and opportunities to practice and apply their knowledge to larger sets of words.

Henderson (1990) and Templeton and Bear (1992) state that students learn about the specific features of words through a developmental process. The hierarchical order for this developmental process is
• learning about sound/symbol relationships
• recognizing spelling patterns in words
• being able to syllabicate words
• understanding the use of affixes
• recognizing root words
• analyzing word origins and derivations

Often, students who have difficulty with the reading process do so because they have little or no understanding of how words are structured and used. Since these students may still be struggling with decoding strategies, they may not have been exposed to multisyllabic words that require them to look at affixes, syllables, and/or word origins. Once students begin to learn the structures of words, their reading, decoding skills, spelling skills, and comprehension and fluency skills improve.

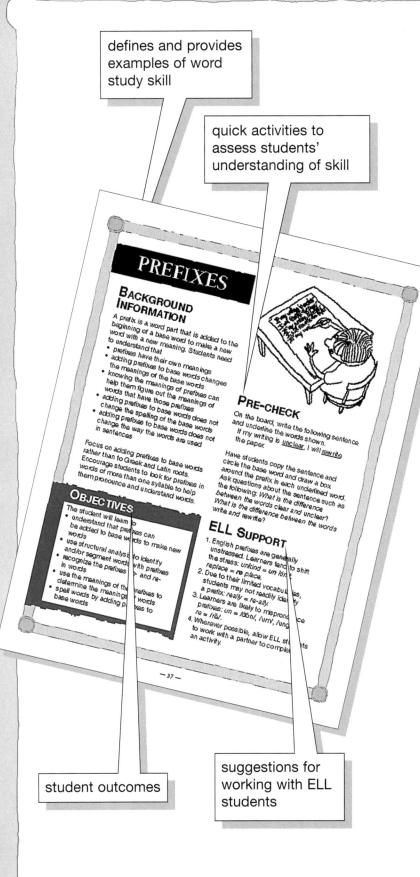

PREFIXES

BACKGROUND INFORMATION

A prefix is a word part that is added to the beginning of a base word to make a new word with a new meaning. Students need to understand that

- prefixes have their own meanings
- adding prefixes to base words changes the meanings of the base words
- knowing the meanings of prefixes can help them figure out the meanings of words that have those prefixes
- adding prefixes to base words does not change the spelling of the base words
- adding prefixes to base words does not change the way the words are used in sentences

Focus on adding prefixes to base words rather than to Greek and Latin roots. Encourage students to look for prefixes in words of more than one syllable to help them pronounce and understand words.

OBJECTIVES

The student will learn to
- understand that prefixes can be added to base words to make new words
- use structural analysis to identify and/or segment words with prefixes
- recognize the prefixes un- and re- in words
- use the meanings of the prefixes to determine the meanings of words
- spell words by adding prefixes to base words

PRE-CHECK

On the board, write the following sentence and underline the words shown. *If my writing is* <u>unclear</u>, *I will* <u>rewrite</u> *the paper.*

Have students copy the sentence and circle the base word and draw a box around the prefix in each underlined word. Ask questions about the sentence such as the following: *What is the difference between the words clear and unclear? What is the difference between the words write and rewrite?*

ELL SUPPORT

1. English prefixes are generally unstressed. Learners tend to shift the stress: *unkind = un /kīn/*, *replace = re /plās/*.
2. Due to their limited vocabularies, students may not readily identify a prefix: *really = re-ally*.
3. Learners are likely to mispronounce prefixes: *un = /ōon/, /um/, /ung/*, *re = /rē/*.
4. Wherever possible, allow ELL students to work with a partner to complete an activity.

— 37 —

TEACHING WITH FAST TRACK READING WORD STUDY

Students need not only direct and explicit instruction in order to learn and understand how words are constructed, but also productive instruction where teaching one set of words leads to learning other words. (Stahl and Stiel 1999)

The instruction sequence for word study in *Fast Track Reading* provides explicit, direct, and productive instruction. Opportunities are provided for students to identify, analyze, and use words with affixes, root words, syllable patterns, word origins, and words with the same, different, or multiple meanings. Students also learn how to identify and determine the meanings of words within meaningful contexts. Each lesson follows the same teaching sequence and has the same teaching components.

1 Before teaching the lesson, the teacher can use the **Pre-check** provided to determine the level of understanding of the students for that particular skill. The teacher can then decide how much time to spend on the preteaching sequence, or whether to move directly into the coach sequence. Several options for the development of the lesson depending on the needs of the students are provided for most skills.

2 During the **Demonstrate** sequence, the teacher preteaches the skill and explicitly models the skill for students.

3 During the **Coach** sequence of the lesson, the teacher and students work together to practice the skill, with the teacher offering guidance and direct instruction as needed. Using **MATCHWORD™**, the teacher can prepare a worksheet that has been developed specifically for the needs and abilities of the students. (See below for more on **MATCHWORD**.)

4 Following the Coach sequence, the students have an opportunity to **Apply** the skill on their own. An Activities Bank provides multiple suggestions for ways that students can apply the skill. Through **MATCHWORD**, the teacher can provide as much application of the skill as students need.

5 The next step is to **Assess** students' understanding of the skill. Informal assessment is provided along with a formal assessment in the form of a blackline master.

6 If the teacher finds that some students need more practice, a **Reteach** section is provided that offers suggestions for further developing the skill.

The lessons provided in the *Word Study Teacher Guide* are generic in that the teacher can use the format to teach any word in that category. This means that the lessons can be customized according to the level of the students. Word lists are provided for many of the lessons to help teachers choose from easy, medium, and hard words. The focus of the lessons is on the concept being taught about the words in the category or set, and students are encouraged to apply

teacher demonstrates and preteaches the skill

teacher and students work together to practice the skill

students work independently or with partners to practice the skill

informal assessment measures to check students' knowledge of skill

activities for students who need extra practice

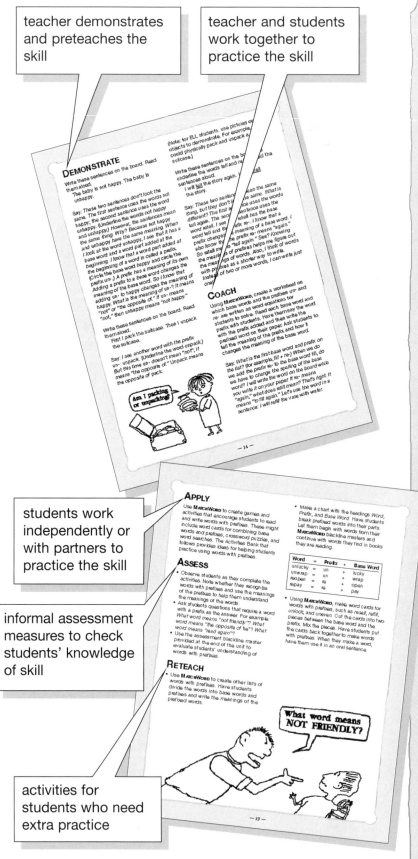

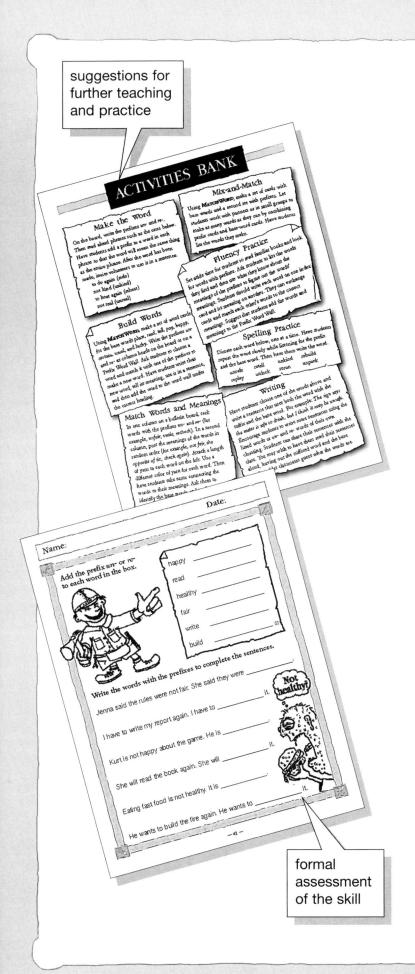

suggestions for further teaching and practice

formal assessment of the skill

this concept to other words in that same set of words. Students reading the *Fast Track* magazines in the Comprehension Strand have the opportunity to apply their understanding of the word concepts to the vocabulary in the stories and articles. An icon references the word study skill in the comprehension teacher guide so that the teacher can use the activities in the *Word Study Teacher Guide* to further enhance the vocabulary teaching for the comprehension lesson.

MATCHWORD

A **MATCHWORD** disc and teacher guide is provided in each *Fast Track* Word Work Strand. **MATCHWORD** is a computer program that allows teachers to create numerous activities that will help them accelerate, extend, reinforce, or remediate their students' learning. Using **MATCHWORD**, teachers can create practice activities for students that are specifically designed for students' needs. Such activities include picture and word cards, letter and word cards, word dice, bingo cards, spinners, word searches, word sorts and word matches, crossword puzzles, sentence strips, cloze sentences, fill in the blank sentences, fill in the bubble activities, and practice texts.

MEETING THE NEEDS OF ELL STUDENTS

The lessons in the *Word Study Teacher Guide* can easily be adapted to meet the needs of English Language Learners (ELL).

When the word study lessons are being presented to ELL students, it is important to note several critical factors:
- What is the level of spoken English for the student?
- Does the student speak oral English with at least an intermediate degree of fluency?
- Does the student speak with a lesser degree of fluency, for example, does he or she speak haltingly, searching for the correct English words or usage?

The Reading/Language Arts Framework for California Public Schools (1999) states that "students must be provided significant support to be successful in the language arts. Such support includes preteaching of essential elements of lesson vocabulary and language structures...."

ELL students can be supported by using specific strategies such as the following:
- Focus on teaching one vocabulary rule at a time
- Have students work with partners or in small groups with other ELL or English Only students
- Provide opportunities to apply new word study strategies through group and independent story, poetry, writing, and drawing
- Provide the necessary background information for students
- Illustrate word meanings with pictures, diagrams, or real objects
- Demonstrate the relationships between words.

As students progress in their acquisition of the English language, they will have an increased understanding and recognition of new vocabulary and word structures.

WORD STUDY ASSESSMENT

The *Fast Track Assessment Guide* provides pre- and post-assessment opportunities for each lesson in each section of the Word Study Strand. These assessments can be given to individual students or used with small groups of students. A score of 4 correct answers out of 5 questions is considered to be a passing score for each assessment item. If the student scores less than 4 out of 5, it is suggested that the teacher provide instruction in that particular word study skill.

Teachers can use the word study assessments to determine the type and amount of instruction that is needed for students. As students progress through the magazines for the different levels in the Comprehension Strand, they encounter more difficult vocabulary. Teachers can reuse the assessments by substituting the vocabulary that the students are reading in the magazines in the Comprehension Strand.

BIBLIOGRAPHY

Adams, M. Jager. (1990). *Beginning to Read: Thinking and Learning About Print*. Cambridge, MA. MIT Press.

Brabham, Edna Greene and Susan Kidd Villaume. (2001). Building Walls of Words. *The Reading Teacher* 54, Vol. 7. 700–712.

Chall, J.S. and H.M. Popp. (1996) *Teaching and Assessing Phonics: A Guide for Teachers*. Cambridge, MA. Educator's Publishing Service.

CORE (2000). *Teaching Reading Sourcebook*. Navato, Col. Arena Press.

Cunningham, P.M. (1995). *Phonics They Use: Words for Reading and Writing*. 2d Ed. New York. Harper Collins College Publishers.

Henderson, E.H. (1990). *Teaching Spelling*. Boston, MA. Houghton Mifflin.

Henry, M.K. (1999). Beyond Phonics: Integrated Decoding and Spelling Instruction Based on Word Origins and Structure. *Read All About It! Readings to Inform the Profession*. Sacramento, CA. California State Board of Education.

Ivernizzi, M.A., M. P. Abouzeid, and J. W. Bloodgood. (1997). "Integrated Word Study: Spelling, Grammar, and Meaning in the Language Arts Classroom. *Language Arts* Vol. 74. 185–192.

Nagy, W.E. (1988).*Teaching Vocabulary to Improve Reading Comprehension*. Newark, DE. International Reading Association.

Nagy, W.E., R.C. Anderson, and P.A. Herman. (1987). Learning Word Meanings from Context During Normal Reading. *American Educational Research Journal* 24, Vol. 237–270.

Reading/Language Arts Framework for California Public Schools: Kindergarten Through Grade Twelve. (1999). Sacramento, CA. California Department of Education.

Stahl, S.A. and T.G. Shiel. (1999). Teaching Meaning Vocabulary: Productive Approaches for Poor Readers. *Read All About It! Readings to Inform the Profession*. Sacramento, CA. California State Board of Education.

Taberski, Sharon. (2000). *On Solid Ground: Strategies for Teaching Reading K–3*. Portsmouth, NH. Heinemann.

Templeton, S. and D. Bear Eds. (1992). *Development of Orthographic Knowledge and the Foundation of Literacy: A Memorial Festschrift for Edmund H. Henderson*. Hillsdale, NJ. Erlbaum,

Winters, Rod. (2001). Vocabulary Anchors: Building Conceptual Connections with Young Readers. *The Reading Teacher* Vol. 54, No. 7. 659–662.

SECTION 1

Changing Word Meanings

PLURALS

BACKGROUND INFORMATION

A plural noun names more than one person, place, or thing. Students need to understand that

- most regular plural nouns are formed by adding -s to the singular noun
- plurals of nouns ending in s, ss, x, z, ch, or sh (sibilants) are formed by adding -es
- there are some nouns whose plurals are formed in irregular ways (*woman/women*, *tooth/teeth*)
- some nouns are the same in the singular and the plural forms (*sheep/sheep, deer/deer*)

The lesson that follows covers the variety of plural forms. You may wish to concentrate on one type at a time to avoid confusion. A logical teaching sequence would be words that add -s or -es, followed by plural forms that require spelling changes (*story/stories*), and then irregular plurals.

OBJECTIVES

The student will learn to
- recognize, read, and form plural nouns ending in -s and -es
- recognize, read, and form plurals of words ending in -y
- recognize, read, and form plurals of words in which f is changed to v
- recognize, read, and form irregular plurals
- spell selected plural nouns

PRE-CHECK

Write the following words on the board: *dog*, *box*, *shelf*, *bush*, *woman*, *lunch*, *baby*, *deer*. Ask students to copy the words in a column on a piece of paper. Then have them write the plural form of each word next to each word in the column. The words represent the different ways plurals are formed and will give you an idea of students' familiarity with forming plurals.

ELL SUPPORT

1. English speakers pronounce -es as /iz/ or /əz/. These endings add an extra syllable: *box/box-es; watch/watch-es; bus/bus-es.*
2. -ies is often pronounced as /ēs/, /ēz/, /is/, /iz/, or /īs/: *flies = fleece, fleas,* /flis/, /fliz/, and /flīs/.
3. -ves creates a tricky consonant cluster (*wives* = /wīvz/). Learners usually compensate by dropping /v/, /s/, or /vz/ or by inserting a vowel sound (*loaves* = /lō və zə/).
4. The pronunciations of irregular plurals must be memorized (*geese, deer, teeth*).

DEMONSTRATE

The Demonstrate section of the lesson is divided into three parts. For some students, regular plurals will be a review. If this is the case, you will move on to Part 2 and Part 3 as appropriate. Other students may need more practice with forming regular plurals. For these students, move on to the Coach section of the lesson and come back to Part 2 and Part 3 on another day when you feel students are ready.

PART 1

Write the following words in two columns on the board—column 1: *cat, apple, door, balloon, girl, desk*; column 2: *bus, dress, box, church, bush*. Model how to add *-s* or *-es* to make plurals.

Say: *These nouns are singular, which means that there is only one of each of these things. I want to make them plural so that there are more than one of each of these things. I need to add* -s *to the words in the first column to make them plural.* (Add *-s* to the words on the board. Read each word.) *The words in the second column are different. I need to add* -es *to them to make them plural. This is because they end in the letters* s, ss, x, ch, *or* sh, *and I know that words that end in these letters need to have* -es *added in order to make them plural.* (Add *-es* to the words on the board. Read each word.)

PART 2

Write the following sentence on the board:
   I like to read stories about wolves.

Underline the words *stories* and *wolves*.

Say: *I know that* stories *is the plural form of* story, *and* wolves *is the plural form of* wolf. (Write the words *story* and *wolf* directly above their corresponding plural forms in the sentence on the board.) Story *ends in* -y. *If I want to make a word that ends in* -y *plural,*

I have to change the y *to* i *and then add* -es. Wolf *ends in* f. *If I want to make a word ending in* f *plural, I have to change the* f *to* v *and then add* -es. (Highlight these letters in the words on the board as you talk about them.)

PART 3

Write the words *woman* and *tooth* in one column on the board and the words *women* and *teeth* in another column.

Say: *There are some words that I can't make plural by adding* -s *or* -es. *There is no rule I can apply and I just have to learn their plural spellings. I know that* woman *and* tooth *are two examples of these kinds of irregular words.*

Write *deer* and *sheep* on the board.

Say: *When I talk about one deer, I use the word* deer. *But when I want to talk about more than one deer, I still use the word* deer. *There are some words that are the same for singular and for plural. I have had to learn which words these are because there is no rule. I know that* sheep *is another example of a word that is the same in singular and in plural.*

Two of us, but we're still deer.

COACH

Using **MATCHWORD**, create a worksheet that lists singular forms of words whose plurals are formed by adding *-s* or *-es*. Be sure you include words that end in *s*, *ss*, *x*, *z*, *ch*, or *sh*. (If you feel students are ready, and you have taken them through Part 2 of the Demonstrate section of the lesson, you will also want to include some examples of words that end in *y* and *f*.) Read each word with students, have them say the plural form, and then ask them to write the plural form next to its singular form. Have students explain how they know whether to add *-s* or *-es* and whether they need to change final letter *y* or *v* before adding the plural ending.

Say: *Let's look at the first word on the list. What is the word?* (for example, *box*) *What is the plural form of this word? The word* box *ends in* x. *What do we add to a word that ends in* x *to make it plural? I will write it on the board while you write it on your paper. Look at the plural word you wrote and then look at the word I have written on the board. Check to see if you have spelled the word on your paper correctly. Let's look at the next word.*

Continue working through the list, helping students to identify the final letters and to decide how to form the plurals.

When you have taken students through Part 3 of the Demonstrate section of the lesson, prepare a list of words that have irregular plurals, using **MATCHWORD**. Include words that are the same in their singular and plural forms. Help students to read, say, and write these irregular plural forms.

Say: *These words have irregular plural forms. Some words have the same spelling for plural and for singular. You will have to learn how to spell them. Let's look at each one, read it, and then decide what the plural form is. I'll help you with the spelling. When we have created our list of plurals, we will keep the list and spend some time every day practicing their spelling until we know them really well.*

APPLY

Use **MATCHWORD** to create games and activities that require students to read and write plural forms of words such as word cards for matching, word puzzles, and cloze paragraphs. The Activities Bank that follows provides ideas for helping students practice using plural forms.

ASSESS

- Observe students as they work with word cards and games.
- Use the completed **MATCHWORD** blackline masters to evaluate students' ability to read and write plurals.
- Use the assessment blackline master provided at the end of the unit on plurals to evaluate students' understanding.

RETEACH

- Work with students to model how to create plurals.
- Allow extra time for students to practice the words on their list of irregular plurals.
- Use **MATCHWORD** to create more practice sheets for students.
- Call attention to plurals in books that students are reading. Discuss how the plurals were formed.
- Have ELL and English Only students work in groups or pairs to complete the above activities.

Three of us, and we're still sheep.

ACTIVITIES BANK

Plural Baseball

Divide students into two teams for a game of plural baseball. "Pitch" a word to a player on one team by writing a singular noun on the board. The player "at bat" comes to the board and writes the plural form of the word. If that player responds correctly, the team earns a run. Then "pitch" a word to the other team. You might vary the play by "pitching" plural nouns and asking players to supply the singular form. Be sure to include nouns that end in *s, ss, x, z, ch, sh, f,* and *y,* as well as nouns whose plural forms are irregular. Play to ten points and then rearrange teams and play again.

Plural Concentration

Using **MATCHWORD**, prepare word cards for singular nouns on one set and their corresponding plural forms on another set. Have students work with a partner to play Concentration in which they match singular and plural nouns.

Plurals Chart

Prepare a chart with the headings "words with *-s,*" "words with *-es,*" "words ending in *-y,*" "words ending in *f,*" and "irregular plurals." Encourage students to look for plurals in their reading. Have them write the words they find under the appropriate heading on the wall chart.

Build Words

Have pairs of students use letter cards created from **MATCHWORD** to build singular and plural nouns. One student can think of a singular noun, form it using the letter cards, and then read it aloud. The other student then forms the plural form of the word.

Spelling Dictation

As students become more familiar with reading and writing plural forms of words, you may want to set up a weekly dictation time with them. Dictate the singular form of a word first. Have students repeat the word and then write it. Then dictate the plural form. Have students repeat the word and write it next to the singular form on their paper.

Cloze Sentences

Using **MATCHWORD**, create cloze paragraphs that include plural words. Have students write the correct form of a plural word that makes sense in the space. More able students can write their own paragraphs and leave spaces where there are plural words. They can exchange their paragraphs and have a partner fill in plural words that make sense in the paragraph.

Writing

Have students write a description of their classroom. Encourage them to use as many plural nouns as they can in their descriptions.

Name: Date:

Write the plural form of each word.

story ______________________

goose ______________________

calf ______________________

church ______________________

dress ______________________

fox ______________________

sheep ______________________

army ______________________

woman ______________________

berry ______________________

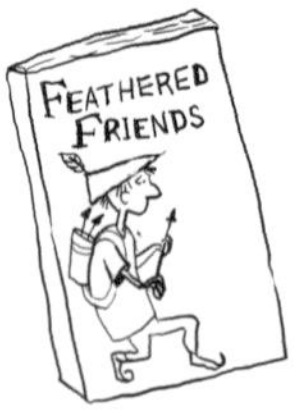
FEATHERED
FRIENDS

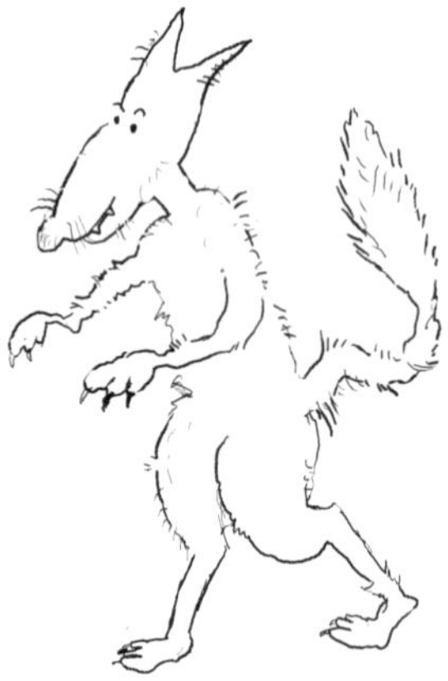

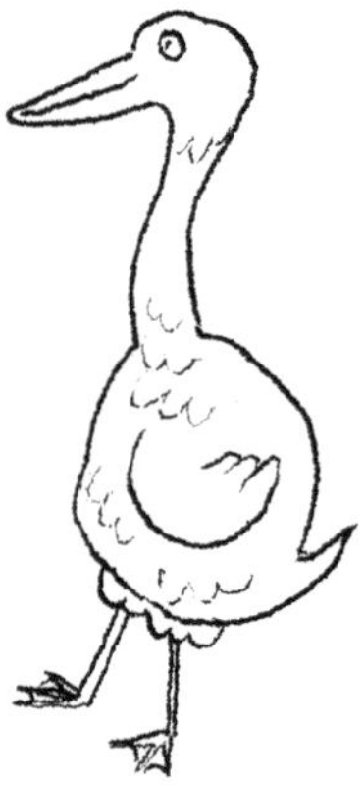

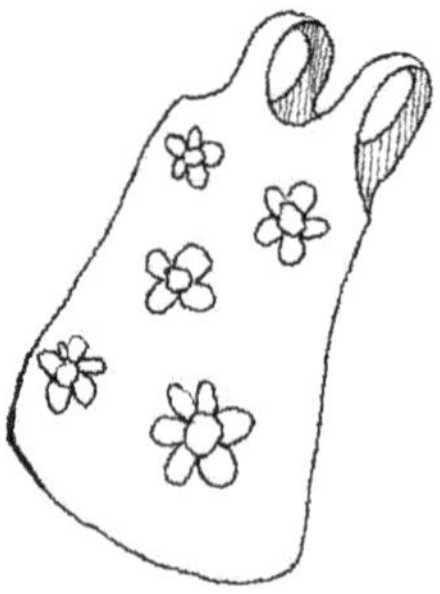

Write the singular form of each plural word.

knives ______________________

cakes ______________________

bakeries ______________________

teeth ______________________

bikes ______________________

brushes ______________________

apples ______________________

frogs ______________________

flies ______________________

loaves ______________________

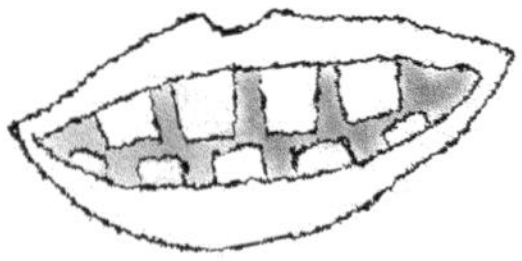

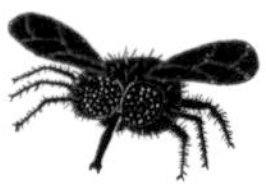

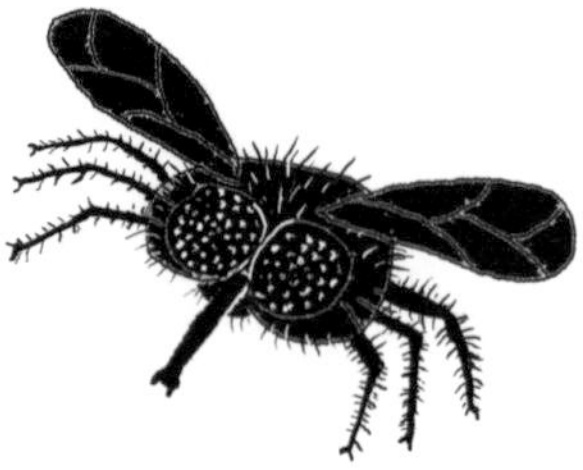

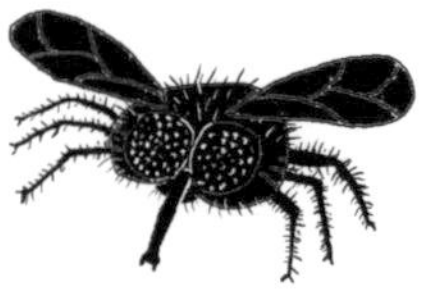

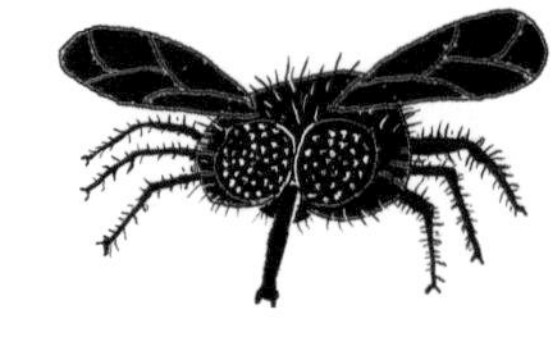

VERB ENDINGS

BACKGROUND INFORMATION

A base word is a word to which endings and affixes can be added. Students need to understand that

- the verb endings -s and -es are added to the base word when one person, animal, or thing does the action, and the action takes place in the present
- the ending -ed shows that the action took place in the past, while the ending -ing shows that the action is continuing
- some base words may require spelling changes (drop final e, double final consonant) before an ending is added

Introduce regular verbs that add endings without spelling changes before teaching verbs that require spelling changes when endings are added.

OBJECTIVES

The student will learn to
- recognize that endings can be added to verbs to make new words
- understand that the meaning of the base word is changed when an ending is added
- recognize, read, and form base words with the endings -s, -es, -ed, and -ing
- spell selected words with the endings -s, -es, -ed, and -ing

PRE-CHECK

Write the following words and endings on the board.

jump	+	-s	laugh	+	-ing
watch	+	-es	smile	+	-ed
play	+	-ed	swim	+	-ing

Ask students to put each word and ending together and write the new word. Then have them use each word in a sentence. Look at how students write the words and listen to how they use the words in context. This will help you gauge their familiarity with adding endings to verbs and using verbs with endings. This is an especially appropriate pre-check for ELL students. It should help you decide whether to focus on one or more verb endings.

ELL SUPPORT

Common pronunciation difficulties:
- -s and -es have four possible pronunciations: /s/, /z/, /iz/, /cz/.
- -ed has four possible pronunciations: /t/, /d/, /id/, /əd/.
- The endings /iz/, /əz/, /it/, and /əd/ add a syllable to the base word: wish vs. wish-es, wait vs. wait-ed. They also create tricky consonant clusters: eats = /ēts/; loves = /luvz/; walked = /wôkt/, hugged = /hugd/.
- For words ending in -ing, learners often substitute /n/ or /m/ or add /k/ or /g/; eating = eatin'/eatim/eating-k/eating-g.

I am Wishing I had wished for a better wish . . .

— 17 —

DEMONSTRATE

The Demonstrate section of the lesson is divided into two parts. Some students may already be familiar with adding endings to verbs with no spelling changes. For these students, move on to Part 2. Other students may benefit from a review of how to add endings to verbs with no spelling changes. If this is the case, after Part 1, move on to the Coach section of the lesson and come back to Part 2 on another day.

PART 1

Write this set of sentences on the board. Underline the verb in each sentence.

> Dan <u>walks</u> home.
> Dan <u>walked</u> home.
> Dan is <u>walking</u> home.

Say: *I see that the base word in these three words is the same—walk. But I also see that* walk *has a different ending in each sentence.* (Circle the endings *-s, -ed,* and *-ing.*) *I know that these endings change the meaning of the word* walk. (Point to each sentence as you talk about it.) *The ending -s tells me that the action is happening right now. The ending -ed tells me that the action happened in the past. The ending -ing tells me that the action is happening now and is continuing.*

Repeat the above process with this set of sentences.

> Marie fixes the car.
> Marie fixed the car.
> Marie is fixing the car.

Say: *I added -es, not -s, to* fix *in the first sentence because* fix *ends in* x. *I remembered that words that end in* s, ss, x, ch, *or* sh *have to have -es instead of -s. I also know that both -s and -es are endings that are added to singular verbs, or verbs that tell about one person or thing. If I wrote about Dan and Marie walking home, I would write* Dan and Marie walk home. (Write the sentence on the board as you say it.) *Because this sentence tells about more than one person, I don't add -s or -es to* walk.

PART 2

Write these words on the board.

> like
> likes
> liked
> liking

Say: *When I added the ending -s to* like, *I didn't have to change the base word, just like with the other words I wrote. But when I added -ed or -ing, I changed the spelling of the base word. I dropped the final* e *before I added the ending.* (Underline the endings *-s, -ed,* and *-ing.*) *Because the endings -ed and -ing begin with a vowel, I had to drop the final* e *in* like.

Continue with other examples, such as *bake, love,* and *use.*

Write these words on the board.

> clap
> claps
> clapped
> clapping

Say: *See? There was no change in the base word* clap *when I added -s. But when I added -ed or -ing, the spelling of the base*

— 18 —

word changed. How? The final consonant was doubled—one p became two p's. Why? Because the ending begins with a vowel, and the base word has one syllable, one vowel, and one final consonant. I think of this as the 1-1-1 rule.

Continue with other examples, such as *swim, grin,* and *hug.*

COACH

Using **MATCHWORD**, create a worksheet that lists regular verbs whose spellings do not change when endings are added. Include verbs that end in *s, ss, ch, sh,* or *x.* Read each verb with students. Ask them how they would change the verb to show that one person is doing that action right now. Have them write the *-s* (or *-es*) form of the verb next to the base word.

Say: *What do we add to a verb so that it tells about one person doing the action right now? That's right. We add either* -s *or* -es. *What is the first verb on the list?* (for example, *dash*) *What does* dash *end with? Do we add* -s *or* -es? *I will write the word on the board while you write it on your paper. Did you write the same word I did? Check to see that you spelled it correctly.*

Continue with the other words in the list. Then go back through the list twice. Have students write the *-ed* forms of the verbs and then the *-ing* forms of the verbs.

After you and the students have completed Part 2 of the Demonstrate section of the lesson, use **MATCHWORD** to create a worksheet of regular verbs whose spellings change (drop the final *e* or double the final consonant) when endings are added. This time ask students to write each verb with the endings *-s, -ed,* and *-ing.* Have them explain how they knew whether a spelling change was needed and if so, what change they made.

Say: *What is the first verb on this list?* (for example, *close*) *If we add* -s *to* close, *does the spelling change? Does the spelling change if we add* -ed *or* -ing? *You write* close *with the endings* -s, -ed, *and* -ing *on your paper while I write them on the board. Then compare what you wrote with what I wrote.*

Continue with the other words on the list.

APPLY

Use **MATCHWORD** to create games and activities that encourage students to read and write verbs with endings. These might include word bingo, crossword puzzles, and cloze sentences. The Activities Bank that follows provides ideas for helping students practice using verbs with endings.

ASSESS

- Watch students as they complete the activities.
- Listen as students explain to a partner how they added endings to verbs on their **MATCHWORD** blackline masters.
- Use the assessment blackline master provided at the end of the unit to evaluate students' understanding of verb endings.

RETEACH

- Use **MATCHWORD** to create more lists of regular verbs to which students can add endings.
- Write word equations (such as *hope – e + ing*) for students to solve.
- Ask students to find and list verbs with endings in books they are reading. Ask them whether or not the base word changed when the ending was added and how it changed.
- Have pairs of students take turns giving each other a base word and an ending to write and checking their work.
- Have ELL students act out or demonstrate base words and their endings. They could also draw a picture and explain it.

ACTIVITIES BANK

Verb Search

Divide students into groups and have them look through a classroom book to find certain kinds of verbs. For the first search, have groups find verbs in which the final *e* was dropped when an ending was added. A second search can focus on verbs in which the final consonant was doubled before an ending was added. Have students list the verbs they find and share them with the class.

Spin an Ending

Make a spinner by dividing a tagboard circle into three sections and labeling the sections *s, es; ed;* and *ing*. Cut out an arrow and attach it loosely to the center of the circle with a brass fastener. Using **MATCHWORD**, prepare a variety of word cards for regular verbs, such as *lock, quack, rake, watch, clap, skate, fill, lick, yell,* and *pack*. In small groups, students take turns drawing a card, spinning an ending for that word, and using the new word in a sentence.

Cloze Sentences

Using **MATCHWORD**, create cloze sentences and word choices such as those below. Read them aloud with students. Have students select the correct word to finish each sentence, write the word in the blank, and read the completed sentence.

A dog _____. (*bark, barks*)
The girls _____. (*run, runs*)
That boy is _____ his dad. (*call, calling*)
When it is broken, Mom _____ the car. (*fix, fixes*)
Miguel _____ the ball. (*kick, kicks*)
Last week I _____ all the way home. (*skip, skipped*)
Carla is _____ her milk. (*drink, drinking*)
We _____ in the garden yesterday. (*work, worked*)

Change Sentences

Write some sentences on tagboard strips and underline the verb in each sentence. Have students choose a sentence strip and copy the sentence. Then have them use the idea of the sentence to write two new sentences containing the underlined word with different endings. For example, the sentence *The plane will land* can be rewritten as *The plane is landing* and *The plane landed*. Have students share their sentences with the class, discuss how they changed the meaning of the original sentence, and tell about any spelling changes they made in the base word.

Spelling Dictation

Dictate to students verbs with the endings *-s, -es, -ed,* and *-ing,* such as those listed below. Have students repeat each word slowly while listening for the ending. Then have them write the word.

jumped	hopped	likes
baking	wishes	opened
swimming	dashes	batted

Writing

Mix the verb word cards from the Spin an Ending activity and place them face down. Have students choose three cards at random. Challenge them to write a short story about something that happened in the past, using all three verbs. Have ELL students dictate a story using the word cards.

Add the word ending to the base words. Write the new words on the lines.

-s		**-es**	
turn	talk	fix	watch
_____	_____	_____	_____
run	shout	wash	push
_____	_____	_____	_____
climb	work	catch	mix
_____	_____	_____	_____

-ed		**-ing**	
jump	grab	laugh	dance
_____	_____	_____	_____
smile	clap	look	shop
_____	_____	_____	_____
start	wave	sit	joke
_____	_____	_____	_____

Select two of your new words from the above list and write a sentence.

_____

_____

COMPARATIVES

BACKGROUND INFORMATION

Adjectives and adverbs can be used to compare. There are three degrees of comparison: positive *(big)*, comparative *(bigger)*, and superlative *(biggest)*. Students need to understand that

- most words of one syllable and some words of two syllables form the comparative and superlative by adding the suffixes *-er* and *-est,* respectively
- the suffix *-er* is used when comparing two things, and the suffix *-est* is used when comparing three or more things
- some base words may require spelling changes (drop final *e,* double final consonant, change *y* to *i)* before adding *-er* or *-est*

Introduce adjectives and adverbs that add *-er* and *-est* without spelling changes before teaching those that require spelling changes when the suffixes are added.

OBJECTIVES

The student will learn to
- understand that the suffixes *-er* and *-est* can be added to base words to make new words
- understand that the suffix *-er* is used when two things are being compared and that the suffix *-est* is used when three or more things are being compared
- recognize, read, and form words with the suffixes *-er* and *-est*
- verbalize a spelling strategy for adding *-er* and *-est* to words
- spell selected words with the suffixes *-er* and *-est*

PRE-CHECK

Write these three cloze sentences on the board.

This pencil is _____.
This pencil is _____ than that one.
This pencil is the _____ of the three.

Write the word *long* to complete the first sentence. Ask students how they can use the word *long* to compare the pencils in the other two sentences. If necessary, offer the words *longer* and *longest* and ask students to use the words to complete the sentences. This will give you an idea of students' familiarity with making comparatives and using them in sentences.

ELL SUPPORT

One of the ways that English forms comparatives and superlatives is by adding *-er* or *-est* to an adjective. This can cause problems because
- Languages compare adjectives differently.
- The *r* in *-er* is difficult for most students. They may drop it or pronounce it as /l/.
- Many languages do not allow consonant clusters. Learners may therefore drop the *s, t,* or *st* in *-est.*
- Suffixes are normally unstressed in English. Students often shift the stress to *-er* or *-est.*
- Spanish speakers do not have the direct transfer of comparatives. For example, *sweet, sweeter, sweetest* would translate *dulce, más dulce,* and *el más dulce.*

DEMONSTRATE

The Demonstrate section of the lesson is divided into two parts. For those students who are already familiar with adding *-er* and *-est* to adjectives with no spelling changes, move on to Part 2. For those students who need more practice adding *-er* and *-est* to adjectives with no spelling changes, go through Part 1, then move on to the Coach section of the lesson. Come back to Part 2 on another day.

PART 1

Draw a circle and next to it, write this sentence and read it aloud:
   This circle is small.

Draw another circle that is slightly smaller than the first circle.

Say: *Now I want to write a sentence that compares this circle* (point to the second circle) *to this circle* (point to the first circle). *I want to use the word* small *again.*

Write this sentence on the board:
   This circle is smaller than that one.
Underline the word *smaller.*

Say: *I used the word* small, *but I had to add a suffix to the word.* (Circle the suffix *-er.*) *When I use an adjective to compare two things, I add* -er *to the end of the adjective. In this sentence, I was comparing these two circles, so I added* -er *to* small.

Draw a third circle that is smaller than either of the others.

Say: *I want to write a sentence about this circle* (point to the third circle) *that compares it to the other two circles. I want to use the word* small *again.*

Write this sentence on the board:
   This circle is the smallest of all.
Underline the word *smallest.*

Say: *I used the word* small *again, but I had to add another suffix to the word.* (Circle the suffix *-est.*) *When I use an adjective to compare three or more things, I add* -est *to the end of the adjective. In this sentence, I was comparing these three circles, so I added* -est *to* small.

PART 2

Write these words in a column on the board:
   nice
   sad
   happy

Say: *Sometimes when I add* -er *or* -est *to an adjective, I have to change the spelling of the base word. Look at the first word:* nice. *If I want to add* -er *or* -est *to* nice, *I have to drop the final* e. *Why? Because the suffixes* -er *and* -est *begin with a vowel.*

Write the words *nicer* and *nicest* next to *nice* on the board. Use each word in a sentence and ask students to identify what and how many things you are comparing. Repeat the process with the words *large* and *blue.*

Say: *Now look at the second word on the list:* sad. *If I want to add* -er *or* -est *to* sad, *I have to double the final consonant* d. *Why? Because* -er *and* -est *begin with a vowel, and* sad *has one syllable, one vowel, and one final consonant. I think of it as the 1-1-1 rule: one syllable, one vowel, one final consonant.*

Write the words *sadder* and *saddest* next to *sad* on the board. Use each word in a sentence and again have students tell you what and how many things you are comparing. Continue with the words *big* and *hot.*

Say: *Look at the last word on the list:* happy. *I want to add* -er *and* -est *to* happy. *What do I have to do to the base word? I have to change the* y *to* i *because* -er *and* -est *begin with a vowel, and* happy *ends with a consonant and a* y.

Write the words *happier* and *happiest* next to *happy* on the board. Offer the words in sentences and have students identify what and how many are being compared. Repeat with the words *merry* and *silly.*

COACH

Using **MATCHWORD**, create a worksheet that lists adjectives that do not change their spelling when *-er* or *-est* is added. (If you have taken students through Part 2 of the Demonstrate section, include adjectives that change their spelling before adding *-er* or *-est.)* Read each adjective with students. Ask them how they would change the adjective if they were using it to compare two things. Have them write the *-er* form of the adjective next to the base word.

Say: *What is the first adjective on the list?* (for example, *slow) If we use* slow *to compare two things, what suffix do we add? I will write the word on the board while you write it on your paper. Look at the word I have written. Did you write it the same way?*

Continue with the other adjectives on the list. Then go back through the list and have students write the *-est* forms of the adjectives.

You may want to use **MATCHWORD** to create a separate worksheet of adjectives that change their spelling (drop the final *e,* double the final consonant, change *y* to *i*) when *-er* and *-est* are added. Ask students to write the *-er* and *-est* forms of the adjectives. Have them explain how they knew what spelling change to make.

Say: *What is the first adjective on the list?* (for example, *fine) What happens to the final* e *when we add* -er *and* -est *to* fine? *I will write the words on the board while you write them on your paper. How did you spell the words?*

Continue with the other adjectives on the list.

APPLY

Use **MATCHWORD** to create games and activities in which students read and write *-er* and *-est* forms of adjectives. Possibilities include word cards for matching, crossword puzzles, and cloze sentences. The Activities Bank that follows provides ideas for helping students practice writing and using *-er* and *-est* forms of adjectives.

ASSESS

- Observe students as they complete the activities. Note in particular whether they know when to use an adjective with *-er* and when to use one with *-est.*
- Point to *-er* and *-est* forms of adjectives that students wrote on their **MATCHWORD** blackline masters. Ask them to use the words in sentences.
- Use the assessment blackline master provided at the end of the unit to evaluate students' understanding of comparatives.

RETEACH

- Write word equations (such as *happy – y + i + er*) for students to solve.
- Use **MATCHWORD** to create cloze sentences for students to complete with *-er* and *-est* forms of adjectives. Provide the adjectives, or let students choose their own.
- Ask students to look for *-er* and *-est* forms of adjectives in their reading. Have them identify what and how many things are being compared.
- Create adjective word cards and suffix *-er* and *-est* cards using **MATCHWORD**. Have students draw an adjective card and a suffix card and tell how they would add the suffix to the adjective.

ACTIVITIES BANK

Riddle Me

Let students play a guessing game using comparisons as clues. The leader gives a clue: *I am thinking of something that is faster than a train but slower than the space shuttle. What is it?* (jet plane) The student who guesses correctly takes a turn as the next leader. You might offer these riddles as models.

I am thinking of an animal that is bigger than a kitten but smaller than a horse.
(Possible answers: dog, fox, wolf, pig, tiger)
I am thinking of the largest animal that lives on land. (elephant)

Fluency Practice

Ask students to collect words with the comparative suffixes *-er* and *-est* from environmental print, magazines, and books. Have them list the words they find and then sort the words according to their spelling patterns. Help students verbalize the spelling generalizations or rules for spelling changes. Keep the word lists available for the addition of new words that students encounter in their reading.

Comparison Puzzles

Have students find pictures in magazines or catalogs that represent comparison sets (for example, tall/taller/tallest, long/longer/longest). Have them paste the pictures side by side on a sheet of paper and print the base word and its *-er* and *-est* forms on the back. As students take turns showing their pictures, classmates can figure out what words the pictures represent.

Put It in Context

Using MATCHWORD, make word cards for words such as *big, bright, quick, sick, wide, light, small, fast, neat, safe, easy,* and *hot.* Divide students into small groups and give one or more word cards to each group. Have group members make up three sentences, using their assigned word and the *-er* and *-est* forms of the word. Suggest that groups write and illustrate their sentences, then share them with the class.

Progressive Pictures

Provide drawing paper, crayons or markers, and word cards for adjectives that you make using MATCHWORD. Divide students into groups of three. Have each group choose a word card and decide on an illustration for the word. One student can illustrate the word on the card, while the other two create illustrations for the word with the suffixes *-er* and *-est.* Students should label their pictures and tape them together to show a progression.

Spelling Dictation

Dictate each of the following words, one at a time. Have students repeat the word slowly while listening for the suffix *-er* or *-est.* Then have them write the word.

bigger	warmest	easier	saddest	shorter
happiest	quicker	hottest	nicer	harder

Writing

Using MATCHWORD, make lists of adjectives, such as *lucky, deep, cold, sleepy, wet, thick, silly,* and *fast.* Divide students into small groups and give each group one of the lists. Ask them to write a story using as many of their words—with the suffix *-er* or *-est* added—as they can. Encourage them to illustrate their stories. Let groups take turns sharing their stories by reading them aloud to the class.

Add *-er* or *-est* to each word to complete the chart.

	-er	-est
windy		
sad		
large		
slow		
tall		

Add *-er* or *-est* to the word in parentheses to complete each sentence.

That box is _____ than this one. (large)

Tuesday was the _____ day of the week. (windy)

Hal is a _____ runner than Dan. (slow)

The giraffe is the _____ animal in the zoo. (tall)

The movie was _____ than the book. (sad)

POSSESSIVES

BACKGROUND INFORMATION

The possessive form is used to show "belonging," or that people, animals, or things have or own something. Students need to understand that

- singular nouns usually form the possessive by adding an apostrophe and an *s*
- irregular plural nouns usually form the possessive by adding an apostrophe and an *s*
- plural nouns that end in *-s, -es,* or *-ies* form the possessive by adding an apostrophe only

Introduce plural nouns before teaching possessives. Also, it is important to help students distinguish between possessives and contractions, since both forms use the apostrophe.

OBJECTIVES

The student will learn to
- understand the print convention of using an apostrophe with an *s* (*'s* or *s'*) to show ownership or possession
- recognize and read singular and plural possessives
- form singular and plural possessives

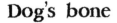
Dog's bone   Dogs' bone

PRE-CHECK

Write these sentences on the board. Underline the possessive nouns.
    The <u>girl's</u> jacket is purple.
    Her <u>brothers'</u> jackets are green.

Ask students why the word *girl* has an apostrophe and an *s* at the end and why the word *brothers* has an apostrophe at the end. How does adding these things to the nouns change their meaning? Use the discussion to see what students know about forming and using possessive nouns.

ELL SUPPORT

1. Possessive forms can be confusing to students acquiring English because their languages may express possessives differently.
   - Students may want to "pronounce" the apostrophe (a potentially foreign symbol).
   - When *'s* and *s'* = /s/ (*Ralph's, the cats'*), students may substitute /sh/, /th/, /z/, or /f/.
   - When *'s* and *s'* = /z/ (*Julia's, the teachers'*), students may substitute /s/, /sh/, /j/, /zh/, /dz/, or /th/.
   - /s/ and /z/ create clusters (*cat's, dogs'*). Learners may drop consonants or add vowels: *dogs* = *dog* or /dos/; *cats* = /ka tə sə/.
2. Wherever possible, use pictures and concrete objects to strengthen vocabulary development.

DEMONSTRATE

The Demonstrate section of the lesson is divided into two parts. Part 1 teaches singular possessives; Part 2 teaches plural possessives. Depending on students' familiarity with singular and plural nouns, you may wish to go through Part 1, then move on to the Coach section of the lesson, and come back to Part 2 on another day.

PART 1

Write these two columns of words on the board.

    Sam   hat
    pen   top

Say: Sam has a hat, The hat belongs to Sam, Sam owns a hat—*I can say any of these sentences to show ownership or possession. But there is a simpler, shorter way to do it. I can say* Sam's hat. *(Write* Sam's hat *on the board and underline the apostrophe and* s*.) If I add an apostrophe and an* s *to the end of* Sam, *I make the word* Sam's. *This is called a possessive noun or a possessive, and it shows that someone has or owns something. Usually the thing that is owned comes right after the possessive. (Point to the possessive phrase* Sam's hat.*) Who owns something?* Sam *does. What does* Sam *own? A hat. The words* Sam's *and* hat *together make a possessive phrase that tells me who or what owns something and what is owned.*
Point to the word *Sam* and then point to the word *pen.*

Say: Sam *is a word that names one person.* Pen *is a word that names one thing.* Sam *and* pen *are both singular nouns. I know that if I want to make a singular noun show ownership, I add an apostrophe and an* s *to the end of the noun. That's what I did to* Sam *to make* Sam's, *and that's what I'll do to* pen *to make* pen's. *(Write* pen's top *on the board and underline the apostrophe and* s.*) What has something? The pen does. What does the pen have? A top. When I see an*

[I am Apostrophe man! I give you the ownership of that car!]

apostrophe and an s *at the end of a noun, I know I should ask myself these questions, "Who or what owns or has something? What does the owner have?"*

PART 2

Write these two columns of words on the board.

    boys   bikes
    babies   toys
    women   shoes

Say: *I know that to make a singular noun—a noun that names one person, place, or thing—show ownership, I add an apostrophe and an* s *to the noun. But what if the noun names more than one person, place, or thing? What if the noun is plural? (Write the possessive phrase* boys' bikes *on the board and draw an arrow pointing to the apostrophe.) To make the word* boys *possessive, I add an apostrophe. Why only an apostrophe? Because* boys *already ends in -s. If a plural noun ends in -s, I add only an apostrophe to make the possessive form.*

Point to the word *babies.*

Say: *The word* babies *is a plural noun, but it ends in -ies, not -s. How will I make the possessive form of* babies? *I will add an apostrophe, just like I did with* boys. *(Write* babies' toys *on the board.) If a plural noun ends in -s, -es, or -ies, I add an apostrophe to make the possessive form.*

— 28 —

Point to the word *women*.

Say: *The word* women *is a plural noun too, but it does not in* -s, -es, *or* -ies. *So I don't make* women *possessive by adding only an apostrophe. I add an apostrophe and an* s, *just like I do with singular nouns.* (Write *women's shoes* on the board and underline the apostrophe and *s.) If a plural noun does not end in* -s, -es, *or* -ies, *I add an apostrophe and an* s *to make the possessive form.*

COACH

Using **MATCHWORD**, create one worksheet that lists singular nouns and one worksheet that lists plural nouns. If you covered singular and plural possessives together, make one worksheet with both singular and plural nouns. Read each word with students, have them say the possessive form, and then have them write the possessive form next to each singular (or plural) noun.

Say: *What is the first word on the list?* (for example, *box) How do we make the word* box *possessive? We know that* box *is a singular noun. What do we add to a singular noun to make its possessive form? I will write the word on the board while you write it on your paper. Did we write the same word? Check to see that you spelled it correctly.*

Continue with the other words on the list, having students identify which are singular or plural (if necessary) and tell how they form the possessives.

APPLY

Use **MATCHWORD** to create games and activities in which students read and write possessive nouns. These games and activities might include letter cards for spelling possessives, word cards for matching nouns and their possessive forms, and cloze sentences to complete with possessives. The Activities Bank that follows provides ideas for helping students practice writing and using possessive nouns.

ASSESS

- Watch students as they complete the games and activities. Check to see that they know how to form the possessives of a singular noun, an irregular plural noun, and a plural noun that ends in *-s.*
- Using **MATCHWORD**, create strips with phrases such as *the wings of a bird, the shoes of the children, the wheels of the bikes.* Distribute the strips to students and have them rewrite the phrase using a possessive noun.
- Use the assessment blackline master provided at the end of the unit to evaluate students' understanding of possessives.

RETEACH

- Give students large sticky notes and have them write possessive phrases to use as labels on classroom objects, for example, *teacher's desk, Liz's chair.*
- Using **MATCHWORD**, write sentences with possessive nouns that are missing an apostrophe. For example, *Jet is the childrens dog.* Ask students to add the apostrophe in the correct place.
- Use sticky notes to mask possessive nouns in a familiar story. As you read the story aloud with students, have them predict what the masked words are. Remove the notes and compare their predictions with the actual story words.
- Divide the class into two teams, the Singulars and the Plurals. Say a noun such as *chair* or *tables.* Depending on whether the word is singular or plural, the Singulars or the Plurals claim the word and write its possessive form on the board.

ACTIVITIES BANK

Form Possessives

Give pairs of students ten index cards. Ask partners to brainstorm ten nouns. (Suggest that they avoid choosing proper nouns.) Have students write the singular possessive form of each noun on one side of a card and the plural possessive form on the other side. Students can share their words with the class.

The Worker's Possession

Ask small groups of students to brainstorm names for workers and things these workers would use. For example, a firefighter would use a hose and an ax. Have students use the words to write possessive phrases, for example, *a firefighter's hose*. If time permits, ask students to draw pictures of the objects to share with the class. Have the class identify who might own the objects.

Change the Phrase

Read each phrase below. Ask students how they can change the phrase using a possessive word. Have volunteers write the possessive phrases on the board and underline the possessive nouns. Finally, have students take turns reading the phrases.

the wig of the pig (the pig's wig)
the rug of the bugs (the bugs' rug)
the hats of the cats (the cats' hats)
the van of the man (the man's van)
the pets of the vet (the vet's pets)
the hens of the men (the men's hens)

Find the Phrases

Write the following paragraph on chart paper or the board. Ask a volunteer to read the first sentence and underline the possessive phrase. Have the volunteer identify who or what owns something and what is owned and tell whether the noun is singular or plural and how the possessive was formed. Continue with the other sentences.

I went to Jan's house. She showed me her dog's new puppies. The puppies' eyes are still closed. The mother's fur is yellow. One puppy's fur is black.

Book Search

Encourage students to look through classroom books for examples of possessives. Have them point out the word they find to a partner and ask the partner to tell whether the possessive is singular or plural.

Spelling

Remind students that the possessive of a singular noun is formed by adding 's. Dictate each phrase below. Have students repeat the phrase slowly. Then have them write the phrase.

| Tom's pen | Amy's fish | Ben's dog |
| teacher's book | store's van | friend's cat |

Then remind students that the possessive of a plural noun is formed by adding either an apostrophe or an apostrophe and an *s*. Dictate each phrase below. Have students repeat the phrase slowly. Then have them write the phrase.

| pigs' tails | geese's wings | mice's feet |
| cats' paws | frogs' eyes | sheep's legs |

Writing

Encourage students to think up imaginative story titles that include possessives. You may wish to provide examples to get them started, such as "Bert's Busy Day" or "Ramona's River Ride." Suggest that students design book covers for their titles. They may enjoy writing stories to go with their titles.

Choose one word from each box. Use both words to make a possessive phrase. Write a sentence using the possessive phrase. The first one is done for you.

Owner	Thing Owned
spiders	dresses
car	~~bone~~
~~dog~~	toys
girls	cover
children	webs
book	horn

I found the dog's bone under the bed.

_____

_____

_____

_____

_____

SUFFIXES

BACKGROUND INFORMATION

A suffix is a word part that is added to the end of a base word to make a new word with a new meaning. Students need to understand that

- some suffixes (such as -y) are added to base words to form adjectives *(lucky)*
- some suffixes (such as -ly) are added to base words to form adverbs *(slowly)*
- some suffixes (such as -er) are added to base words to form nouns *(farmer)*
- some base words may require spelling changes (drop final *e,* double final consonant, change *y* to *i)* before adding suffixes

Introduce base words that add suffixes without spelling changes before teaching those that require spelling changes before adding suffixes.

OBJECTIVES

The student will learn to
- understand that suffixes can be added to base words to make new words
- recognize the suffixes -y, -ly, and -er in words and how they change the meanings of base words
- identify base words and suffixes in words
- spell words by adding suffixes to base words

PRE-CHECK

On the board, write the following sentence and underline the words shown.
> The <u>worker</u> <u>quickly</u> cleaned up the <u>messy</u> room.

Read the sentence aloud, then have students read it with you. Ask them what they notice about the words *worker, quickly,* and *messy.* Have volunteers circle the base word and draw a box around the suffix in each word. Ask questions about the sentence such as the following: *Who cleaned up the room? What is a worker? How did the worker clean up the room? What does* quickly *mean? What word describes the room? What word might describe the room after the worker cleaned it up?*

ELL SUPPORT

Some learners may drop certain suffixes. Others may stress or overpronounce them.

Pronunciation problems: -ly, -y
- /l/ = /r/: *quickly = quickry*
- -y = /ī/: *slowly = /slolī/*
- -y is dropped: *easy = ease*

Pronunciation problems: -er
- r is dropped, altered, or substituted by /l/
- -er is not reduced to the quick /ər/

DEMONSTRATE

The Demonstrate section of the lesson is divided into two parts. If students are already familiar with adding suffixes to base words without spelling changes, move on to Part 2. Other students may benefit from a review of how to add suffixes to base words without spelling changes. For those students, go through Part 1, then move on to the Coach section of the lesson. Come back to Part 2 on another day. (Note: For ELL students, you may wish to teach -*ly* and -*er* at different times, depending on students' level of proficiency in English.)

PART 1

Write these sentences on the board and read them aloud.

The sun is bright. The sun shone brightly.

Say: *Both of these sentences tell me about the sun. I see the adjective* bright *in the first sentence.* (Underline the word *bright.*) *I see the word* bright *in the second sentence too, but it has* -ly *at the end. I know that a word part added to the end of a base word is called a* suffix. (Underline the word *bright* and circle the suffix -*ly.*) *In the first sentence,* bright *describes the sun. In the second sentence,* brightly *tells how the sun shone. Adding a suffix to the end of a word changes the meaning of the word. Adding* -ly *to* bright *made the adverb* brightly *and changed the meaning of the word to "in a bright way."*

Write these sentences on the board and read them aloud.

Ali has good health. She is healthy.

Say: *I see the word* health *in the first sentence.* (Underline the word *health.*) *I see the word* health *in the second sentence, but it is different there. It has the suffix* -y. *I know that adding suffixes changes how words can be used and what they mean. In the first sentence,* health *names something Ali has. In the second sentence,* healthy *describes Ali. If*

I add -y *to* health, *I make the adjective* healthy *and I change the meaning of the word to "having health."*

Write these sentences on the board and read them aloud.

Leon can teach. He is a teacher.

Say: *What is the difference between these two words?* (Underline the words *teach* and *teacher.*) *I see that* teacher *has the suffix* -er *added to the base word* teach. *In the first sentence,* teach *tells what Leon does. In the second sentence,* teacher *names a person who teaches. If I add* -er *to* teach, *I make the noun* teacher *and I change the meaning of the word to "a person who teaches."*

PART 2

Write these words on the board.

happy	happily
bake	baker
fun	funny

Say: *I know that sometimes when I add an ending or a suffix to a base word, I have to change the spelling of the base word. That's what happens with these words.* (Point to each pair of words in turn.) *Before I add* -ly *to* happy, *I change the final* y *to* i. *Why? Because words that end in* y, *like* happy, *change the* y *to* i *before adding a suffix. Before I add* -er *to* bake, *I drop the final* e. *Why? Because words that have a final* e, *like* bake, *drop the* e *before adding a suffix that begins with a vowel, like* -er. *Before I add* -y *to* fun, *I double the final consonant* n. *Why? Because words that have a single vowel and a single final consonant, like* fun, *double the final consonant before adding a suffix that begins with a vowel, and when it's a suffix,* -y *is considered a vowel. But changing the spellings of the base words doesn't change anything else: When I add suffixes, I change how I can use the words in sentences and I change what they mean.*

COACH

Using **MATCHWORD**, create a worksheet on which base words and the suffixes *-y, -ly,* and *-er* are written as word equations for students to solve. (If students have completed only Part 1, choose base words that do not require spelling changes. If they have completed both Parts 1 and 2 or only Part 2, include base words whose spellings change when suffixes are added.) Read each base word and suffix with students. Have them say the word with the suffix added and then write the suffixed word on their paper. Ask students whether they had to make any spelling changes and, if so, what spelling changes they made and why.

Say: *Let's look at the first base word and suffix on the list.* (for example, *report + -er) What do we do when we add the suffix -er to the base word* report? *Do we have to change the spelling of the base word? I will write* reporter *on the board while you write it on your paper. Then compare what you wrote with what I wrote to see that you spelled the word correctly.*

APPLY

Use **MATCHWORD** to create games and activities that encourage students to read and write words with suffixes. These might include word bingo, crossword puzzles, and cloze sentences. The Activities Bank that follows provides ideas for helping students practice using words with suffixes.

ASSESS

- As students complete the above games and activities, observe whether they recognize the meanings of words with suffixes and whether they use the words correctly in sentences.
- Ask students questions that require a word with a suffix as the answer. For example: *What word means "a person who leads"? What word means "feeling thirst"? What word means "in a loud way"?*
- Use the assessment blackline master provided at the end of the unit to evaluate students' understanding of words with suffixes.

RETEACH

- Ask pairs of students to find words with the suffixes *-y, -ly,* and *-er* in books they are reading. Suggest that they list each word, writing the base word in one color and the suffix in another color.
- Model reading a book and say: *I read. I am a ___.* Ask students to complete the sentence with the appropriate suffixed word: *I am a reader.* Continue with other actions or conditions, such as speaking quietly, walking slowly, being thirsty, being sleepy, being a singer, being a dancer. Have ELL students act out the sentences.
- Write *-y, -ly,* and *-er* as headings on the board. Write the base words *luck, rain, brave, easy, speak,* and *farm* in a column to the left of the headings. Ask students which suffix can be added to each base word to make a real word. Have them take turns writing the words with suffixes and using them in oral sentences. ELL students can write the sentences and draw pictures to illustrate them.

ACTIVITIES BANK

Analyze Words

On the board or on chart paper, create a chart such as the one that follows, writing only the words in the first column. Have a volunteer read a word, name the base word and the suffix, and write both in the chart. Use the words below and others.

Word	=	Base Word	+	Suffix
sadly	=	sad	+	ly
dreamer	=	dream	+	er
cloudy	=	cloud	+	y

Color-Coded Words

Using **MATCHWORD**, write pairs of related sentences, such as those below. Use a base word in one sentence and the base word with a suffix in the other sentence. Have students read the sentences aloud and, using colored markers, underline the base word in the first sentence and the base word + the suffix in the second sentence.

The wind blew hard. It was windy.
Nina has a soft voice. She talks softly.
Jose can sing. He is a singer.

Suffix Riddles

Ask riddles such as those below to give students practice adding suffixes to change word meaning. Explain that the answer to each riddle is a word with a suffix. Ask volunteers to write the answers on the board and to underline the suffixes.

I am someone who paints. Who am I?
(a painter)
What word with a suffix describes how I am walking? (slowly)
What word describes a day of snow? (snowy)

Adapt this activity for ELL students by having them draw or cut out pictures to illustrate riddles. Have them write their sentences and then work in pairs to read their riddles to one another.

Suffix Puzzles

On tagboard strips, write words such as the following: *messy, rainy, sleepy, brightly, quietly, quickly, speaker, walker, thinker.* Leave space between the base word and the suffix. Make an irregular cut between the base word and the suffix to form two pieces of a puzzle. Cut each word differently. Have pairs of students find the suffixes and base words that go together, write the complete words, and read them.

ACTIVITIES BANK

Mix-and-Match Words

Divide students into small groups. For each group, use **MATCHWORD** to make one set of cards with base words and a second set with suffixes. Ask students to make as many new words as they can in a given time period by combining base-word cards and suffix cards. Have one member of each group act as recorder and write the words the group makes. Begin with the suffixes *-y, -ly,* and *-er* and the base words *rock, dirt, loud, brave, read,* and *travel.*

Suffix Concentration

Using **MATCHWORD**, make two sets of cards—one set for words with suffixes, the other with the words' meanings. For example, *quietly, in a quiet way.* Have pairs of students use the cards to play Concentration. Players place the cards face down, then turn over two cards at a time, trying to match words with their meanings.

Rewrite Sentences

Use **MATCHWORD** to make sentence strips. Write sentences such as those below and underline words to which suffixes can be added. Have students choose a strip and copy the sentence. Ask them to use the idea of the sentence to write a new sentence using the underlined word with a suffix. Encourage students to share their sentences with the class.

My room is a <u>mess</u>. (My room is messy.)
The band played in a <u>loud</u> way. (The band played loudly.)
She is a person who likes to <u>walk</u>. (She is a walker.)

Spelling Challenge

Remind students that sometimes they have to change the spelling of a base word before they add a suffix. Dictate the following words, one at a time. Have students repeat the word slowly while listening for the suffix, then write the word.

happily	noisy
funny	swimmer
driver	shopper
easily	gently

WORD LIST

Suffixes

	-able	-ful, -less	-ion, -tion, -ation	-ness, -ment
Easy	reasonable respectable	beautiful careful helpful painful useful careless helpless painless useless	action direction location imagination invention preparation	business darkness goodness happiness kindness sadness enjoyment government movement payment
	-able	**-ful, -less**	**-ion, -tion, -ation**	**-ness, -ment**
Medium	acceptable comfortable miserable noticeable profitable valuable	cheerful colorful doubtful fearful forceful peaceful powerful endless fearless homeless restless worthless	celebration civilization combination connection construction decoration education election exploration invitation observation operation production	awareness fitness loneliness readiness weakness amusement arrangement equipment excitement improvement management
	-able, -ible	**-ful, -less**	**-ion, -tion, -ation**	**-ness, -ment**
Hard	desirable predictable notable reliable accessible flexible reversible sensible	delightful graceful meaningful plentiful boundless countless thoughtless tireless	association conversation discussion examination information introduction occupation promotion reaction transportation	cleverness emptiness freshness achievement amazement development employment

Add one of the suffixes -*y*, -*ly*, or -*er* to each word in the box. You may have to change the spelling of the base word.

write _____

dirt _____

slow _____

dance _____

gentle _____

sun _____

Write the words with the suffixes to complete the sentences.

This is a very hot job!

The sun was shining. It was a _____ day.

She knows how to dance. She is a good _____.

A snail is slow. It moves _____.

Why is everybody always picking on me?

He likes to write. He wants to be a _____.

Be gentle with the kitten. Pat it _____.

They played in the dirt. They got _____.

PREFIXES

BACKGROUND INFORMATION

A prefix is a word part that is added to the beginning of a base word to make a new word with a new meaning. Students need to understand that

- prefixes have their own meanings
- adding prefixes to base words changes the meanings of the base words
- knowing the meanings of prefixes can help them figure out the meanings of words that have those prefixes
- adding prefixes to base words does not change the spelling of the base words
- adding prefixes to base words does not change the way the words are used in sentences

Focus on adding prefixes to base words rather than to Greek and Latin roots. Encourage students to look for prefixes in words of more than one syllable to help them pronounce and understand words.

OBJECTIVES

The student will learn to
- understand that prefixes can be added to base words to make new words
- use structural analysis to identify and/or segment words with prefixes
- recognize the prefixes *un-* and *re-* in words
- use the meanings of the prefixes to determine the meanings of words
- spell words by adding prefixes to base words

PRE-CHECK

On the board, write the following sentence and underline the words shown.

    If my writing is <u>unclear</u>, I will <u>rewrite</u> the paper.

Have students copy the sentence and circle the base word and draw a box around the prefix in each underlined word. Ask questions about the sentence such as the following: *What is the difference between the words* clear *and* unclear? *What is the difference between the words* write *and* rewrite?

ELL SUPPORT

1. English prefixes are generally unstressed. Learners tend to shift the stress: *unkind = **un** kind; replace = **re** place.*
2. Due to their limited vocabularies, students may not readily identify a prefix: *really = re-ally.*
3. Learners are likely to mispronounce prefixes: *un = /ŏŏn/, /um/, /ung/; re = /rē/.*
4. Wherever possible, allow ELL students to work with a partner to complete an activity.

DEMONSTRATE

Write these sentences on the board. Read them aloud.

The baby is not happy. The baby is unhappy.

Say: *These two sentences don't look the same. The first sentence uses the words* not happy; *the second sentence uses the word* unhappy. *(Underline the words* not happy *and* unhappy.) *However, the sentences mean the same thing. Why? Because* not happy *and* unhappy *have the same meaning. When I look at the word* unhappy, *I see that it has a base word and a word part added at the beginning. I know that a word part added at the beginning of a word is called a* prefix. *(Circle the base word* happy *and circle the prefix* un-.) *A prefix has a meaning of its own. Adding a prefix to a base word changes the meaning of the base word. So I know that adding* un- *to* happy *changes the meaning of* happy. *What is the meaning of* un-? *It means "not" or "the opposite of." If* un- *means "not," then* unhappy *means "not happy."*

Write these sentences on the board. Read them aloud.

First I pack the suitcase. Then I unpack the suitcase.

Say: *I see another word with the prefix* un-: unpack. *(Underline the word* unpack.) *But this time* un- *doesn't mean "not"; it means "the opposite of." Unpack means the opposite of* pack.

Am I packing or unpacking?

(Note: For ELL students, use pictures or real objects to demonstrate. For example, you could physically pack and unpack a real suitcase.)

Write these sentences on the board and underline the words *tell* and *retell.* Read the sentences aloud.

I will <u>tell</u> the story again. I will <u>retell</u> the story.

Say: *These two sentences mean the same thing, but they don't look the same. What is different? The first sentence uses the words* tell again. *The second sentence uses the word* retell. *I see that* retell *has the base word* tell *and the prefix* re-. *I know that a prefix changes the meaning of a base word. I also know that the prefix* re- *means "again." So* retell *means "tell again." See? Knowing the meanings of prefixes helps me figure out the meanings of words. Also, I think of words with prefixes as a shorter way to write. Instead of two or more words, I can write just one!*

COACH

Using **MATCHWORD**, create a worksheet on which base words and the prefixes *un-* and *re-* are written as word equations for students to solve. Read each base word and prefix with students. Have them say the word with the prefix added and then write the prefixed word on their paper. Ask students to tell the meaning of the prefix and how it changes the meaning of the base word.

Say: *What is the first base word and prefix on the list?* (for example, *fill + re-*) *When we add the prefix* re- *to the base word* fill, *do we have to change the spelling of the base word? I will write the word on the board while you write it on your paper. If* re- *means "again," what does* refill *mean? That's right. It means "to fill again." Let's use the word in a sentence: I will refill the vase with water.*

APPLY

Use **MATCHWORD** to create games and activities that encourage students to read and write words with prefixes. These might include word cards for combining base words and prefixes, crossword puzzles, and word searches. The Activities Bank that follows provides ideas for helping students practice using words with prefixes.

ASSESS

- Observe students as they complete the activities. Note whether they recognize words with prefixes and use the meanings of the prefixes to help them understand the meanings of the words.
- Ask students questions that require a word with a prefix as the answer. For example: *What word means "not friendly"? What word means "the opposite of* tie*"? What word means "read again"?*
- Use the assessment blackline master provided at the end of the unit to evaluate students' understanding of words with prefixes.

RETEACH

- Use **MATCHWORD** to create other lists of words with prefixes. Have students divide the words into base words and prefixes and write the meanings of the prefixed words.

- Make a chart with the headings *Word, Prefix,* and *Base Word.* Have students break prefixed words into their parts. Let them begin with words from their **MATCHWORD** blackline masters and continue with words they find in books they are reading.

Word	=	Prefix	+	Base Word
unlucky	=	un	+	lucky
unwrap	=	un	+	wrap
reopen	=	re	+	open
repay	=	re	+	pay

- Using **MATCHWORD**, make word cards for words with prefixes, such as *resell, refill, unlock,* and *uneven.* Cut the cards into two pieces between the base word and the prefix. Mix the pieces. Have students put the cards back together to make words with prefixes. When they make a word, have them use it in an oral sentence.

What word means NOT FRIENDLY?

ACTIVITIES BANK

Make the Word

On the board, write the prefixes *un-* and *re-*. Then read aloud phrases such as the ones below. Have students add a prefix to a word in each phrase so that the word will mean the same thing as the entire phrase. After the word has been made, invite volunteers to use it in a sentence.

to do again (redo)
not kind (unkind)
to heat again (reheat)
not real (unreal)

Build Words

Using **MATCHWORD**, make a set of word cards for the base words *place, read, tell, pay, happy, certain, usual,* and *lucky.* Write the prefixes *un-* and *re-* as column heads on the board or on a Prefix Word Wall. Ask students to choose a word and match it with one of the prefixes to make a new word. Have students write their new word, tell its meaning, use it in a sentence, and then add the word to the word wall under the correct heading.

Match Words and Meanings

In one column on a bulletin board, tack words with the prefixes *un-* and *re-* (for example, *unfair, untie, recheck*). In a second column, post the meanings of the words in random order (for example, *not fair, the opposite of tie, check again*). Attach a length of yarn to each word on the left. Use a different color of yarn for each word. Then have students take turns connecting the words to their meanings. Ask them to identify the base words and prefixes.

Mix-and-Match

Using **MATCHWORD**, make a set of cards with base words and a second set with prefixes. Let students work with partners or in small groups to make as many words as they can by combining prefix cards and base-word cards. Have students list the words they make.

Fluency Practice

Set aside time for students to read familiar books and look for words with prefixes. Ask students to list the words they find and then use what they know about the meanings of the prefixes to figure out the words' meanings. Students should write each word on one index card and its meaning on another. They can exchange cards and match each other's words to the correct meanings. Suggest that students add the words and meanings to the Prefix Word Wall.

Spelling Practice

Dictate each word below, one at a time. Have students repeat the word slowly while listening for the prefix and the base word. Then have them write the word.

unsafe	retell	unkind	rebuild
replay	unlock	rerun	unpack

Writing

Have students choose one of the words above and write a sentence that uses both the word with the suffix and the base word. For example: *The sign says the water is safe to drink, but I think it may be unsafe.* Encourage students to write more sentences using the listed words or *un-* and *re-* words of their own choosing. Students can share their sentences with the class. You may wish to have them read their sentences aloud, leaving out the suffixed word and the base word, and let classmates guess what the words are.

WORD LIST

Prefixes

	in-, im-, il-, ir-	dis-	non-	mis-	over-
Easy	illegal imperfect inactive incorrect	disagree disappear dislike displease disuse	nonfat nonliving nonstop	misguided misplace misprint misspell misunderstand	overcook overdo oversee overthrow overuse
	in-, im-, il-, ir-	**dis-**	**non-**	**mis-**	**over-**
Medium	immortal impersonal impolite impossible improper independent inexpensive insecure irresponsible	disabled discontinue dishonest disobey disorder distrust	nonpoisonous nonprofit	misbehave misconduct mismatch mistreat misuse	overhead overlook overpay oversleep overseas overwork
	in-, im-, il-, ir-	**dis-**	**non-**	**mis-**	**over-**
Hard	illogical immature immobile impatient impractical incapable inconvenient infinite informal irregular irresistible	disadvantage disapprove disarrange disassemble discomfort	nonbreakable nonfiction nonsense	misadventure misfortune misinform mislead mismanage	overcharge overflow overload overpower overtake

Add the prefix *un-* or *re-* to each word in the box.

happy   _____

read   _____

healthy   _____

fair   _____

write   _____

build   _____

Write the words with the prefixes to complete the sentences.

Jenna said the rules were not fair. She said they were _____.

I have to write my report again. I have to _____ it.

Kurt is not happy about the game. He is _____.

She will read the book again. She will _____ it.

Eating fast food is not healthy. It is _____.

He wants to build the fire again. He wants to _____ it.

Not healthy?

SECTION 2

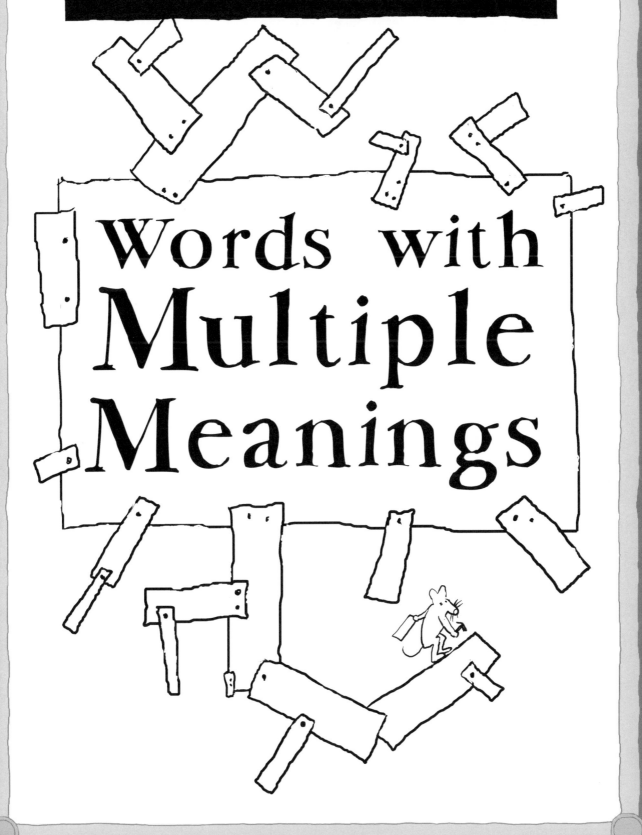

Words with Multiple Meanings

HOMOPHONES

BACKGROUND INFORMATION

Homophones are words that sound the same but have different spellings and different meanings, as in *son* and *sun.* This lesson focuses on twelve pairs of homophones that students are most likely to encounter in their reading: *be/bee, our/hour, blue/blew, see/sea, here/hear, road/rode, cent/sent, new/knew, no/know, right/write, one/won, eight/ate.* However, the lesson can be extended to include additional homophone pairs as well as three-word homophone sets (*where/wear/ ware, or/oar/ore, pair/pear/pare*) or homophone sets that include contractions (*there/their/they're, its/it's*).

OBJECTIVES

The student will learn to
- understand that words with the same pronunciation but different spellings and meanings are called homophones
- recognize and read homophones
- use context clues to determine the meanings of selected homophones
- spell selected homophones

PRE-CHECK

Write the following sentence on the board and read it aloud. Reread the sentence and invite students to read it with you.
    I can't believe I ate eight apples.

Underline the words *ate* and *eight*, and ask students to tell how the words are the same. Then ask how they are different. Invite volunteers to give the meanings of *ate* and *eight.* Ask students to list any other words they know that have the same sounds but different spellings and meanings. How students handle this word pair and others like it will give you an idea of their familiarity with homophones.

ELL SUPPORT

Although homophones can be challenging for all students, learners of English are at a special disadvantage because their limited vocabularies make them less able to recognize the contextual cues that distinguish such pairs as *see* and *sea.* You can help students distinguish and absorb the unusual spelling patterns by writing in the same color chalk words that sound alike *(red/read).* Where applicable, you can use pictographs and visual supports to demonstrate the difference between the words.

Demonstrate

The Demonstrate section of the lesson is divided into three parts. For those students who are already familiar with homophones and can recognize those taught in this lesson, move on to Part 2. For those students who need to learn what homophones are and practice recognizing them, go through Part 1 and proceed to Part 2 when you are sure students have mastered these skills. Part 3 focuses on special homophones that involve contractions.

Part 1

Write the rhyme "A Fly and a Flea in a Flue" on the board:

> A fly and a flea in a flue
> Were trapped, so what could they do?
> Said the fly, "Let us flee!"
> "Let us fly!" said the flea.
> And they flew through a flaw in the flue.

Read the rhyme aloud to students. Through modeling, highlight the words in the rhyme that sound the same but are very different.

Say: *This rhyme has words that sound exactly the same. However, I notice that the words are not spelled the same. For example,* flee *and* flea *sound the same but are spelled differently.* (Write the two words on the board. Say each word. Underline the letters that are different in each word.) *I also know that these two words have very different meanings.* Flee *means "to run away."* A flea *is a tiny insect. Another pair of words like this are* flue *and* flew. (Add these words to the board, say them aloud, and underline the differences in spelling.) *These two words have different spellings and meanings, although they sound the same. A* flue *is a tube or pipe to let out hot air or smoke from a chimney.* Flew *is the past tense of* fly. *Words that sound the same but have different spellings and meanings, as these words do, are called* homophones. *The word*

homophone *helps me remember this idea. The first part,* homo, *means same. The second part of the word,* phone, *means sound.*

Part 2

Write the following sentence on the board: *A blue flag blew in the breeze.* Underline *blue* and *blew* and identify them as homophones. Model how to use context to figure out the meaning of each homophone.

Say: *This sentence has two words that sound the same but are spelled differently and have different meanings. I know that* blue *and* blew *are homophones. I can tell from the overall meaning of the sentence that* blue *must describe the flag and* blew *tells what the flag is doing. I know from experience that we often describe things by color, and* blue *is a describing word that identifies the color of something. I also know from experience that a breeze makes a flag wave and flutter in the air, so* b-l-e-w *means "waved and fluttered."* (Write the sentence *Gina wore a ___ dress* below the first sentence and read it aloud.) *I need to choose one of the homophones for this sentence. I need the homophone that could be used to describe a dress.* Blue *is a color, so* b-l-u-e *is the homophone that fits in this sentence.*

Part 3

Write the following sentence on the board: *You're dragging your jacket.* Underline *you're* and *your*.

Say: *Some homophone pairs have one contraction. I know that contractions are formed by replacing one or more letters of a word with an apostrophe. The contraction* you're *is the same as the words* you are. *I can tell what a contraction means by changing it back into two words and placing them in the sentence.* (Write *You are dragging your jacket.*) *I know that* your *is a possessive pronoun. It means "belonging to you."* Your jacket *means "the jacket that belongs to you." I can study sentences that use one of these homophones to see if the context calls for the contraction or for showing ownership.*

COACH

Using **MATCHWORD**, create a worksheet that lists pairs of homophones. Be sure you include the pairs *be/bee, our/hour, blue/blew, see/sea, here/hear, road/rode, cent/sent, new/knew, no/know, right/write, one/won, eight/ate*. (If you feel students are ready and you have taken them through Part 2 of the Demonstrate section, you will also want to include a cloze sentence that asks for a homophone from each pair. If you have chosen to use Part 3 of the Demonstrate, you may wish to add *it's/its, your/you're*, and *their/there/they're* to your worksheet.) Read each pair of homophones with students, have them spell each one, and talk about its meaning. Then have students read the sentences and fill in the blanks. Ask them to explain how they know which homophone goes in each blank.

Say: *Let's look at the first pair of homophones on the list. What are the words?* (for example, *be/bee*) *How are these words different in spelling? How are these words different in meaning? Let's look at sentence 1 on the bottom half of the sheet.* (for example, *The party will ___ great fun.*) *Which homophone fits in this sentence? Does* be, *the verb, or* bee, *the insect, make sense in the sentence? Write the homophone in the sentence. Now let's look at the next pair of homophones.*

Continue through the list, helping students identify the differences in spelling and meaning and use the context to choose the appropriate word. For ELL students, use pictographs to demonstrate the difference in meaning. Where appropriate, students can act out the words.

APPLY

Use **MATCHWORD** to create games and activities that require students to identify and spell homophones and use context to determine their meanings. For example, you might make word cards, crossword puzzles, Go Fish cards, and mini sentence strips. The Activities Bank that follows provides ideas for helping students practice using homophones.

ASSESS

- Observe students as they complete the activities. Note whether they are able to identify the differences in spelling and meaning in each pair of homophones.
- Point out homophones that students used in their **MATCHWORD** blackline masters. Ask them to use each homophone appropriately in a sentence of their own.
- Use the assessment blackline master provided at the end of the unit to evaluate students' understanding of homophones.

RETEACH

- Write a homophone pair on the board. Read students a sentence using one of the homophones. Have them listen for context clues, then tell the spelling of the homophone that fits. Continue with other pairs.
- Point out homophones in students' reading. Help them spell both homophones and tell the meaning of the homophone used in the selection.
- Allow extra time for students to practice spelling and using the pairs of homophones on their list in context.
- Use **MATCHWORD** to create a worksheet with pictures that illustrate different homophones. Have students use a word bank to select the homophone that matches each picture, then make up a sentence using the word in context.

ACTIVITIES BANK

Use Context Clues

Using **MATCHWORD**, make homophone cards, with one word on each card, and distribute them to students. Have students locate their homophone partner. Say oral sentences that use the homophones. Make sure that you supply context clues that enable students to discern which meaning/homophone you are using. When partners agree on the word, have the student who is holding the word you are using in each sentence stand and spell the word.

Cloze Sentences

Write pairs of cloze sentences like the ones below on the board with a choice of homophones students can use to complete the sentences. Use different colors of chalk to draw the blank lines in each pair of sentences. Invite students to come to the board and use the same color chalk as the blank line to circle the word that correctly completes each sentence.

be, bee	Will you _____ at the party?
	I got stung by a _____.
know, no	I do not _____ how to play chess.
	Please don't say _____.
knew, new	I will wear my _____ shoes tomorrow.
	I _____ the answer to the question.
road, rode	They are paving the _____ into town.
	I _____ my bike to school today.

Go Fish

Create a set of homophone cards using **MATCHWORD**. Give the same number of cards to each student. Place the remaining cards in a center pile. In turn, each player asks another for the match to a homophone in his or her hand. If the other student does not have the matching homophone, the player draws from the center pile. When a player finds a match, he or she displays those cards face up on the table. Players may challenge if they do not think the two words are homophones. Play continues until one student runs out of cards and wins. As an alternative, have students play until all are out of cards; the winner is the player with the most matching pairs.

Secret Messages

Use **MATCHWORD** to make sentence strips with secret messages that have incorrect spellings for homophones. For example: *Please by sum flours at the sail.* (Please buy some flowers at the sale.) *Bee a deer and right you're grandmother.* (Be a dear and write your grandmother.) Pair students and give each pair one secret message to decode by substituting homophones.

ACTIVITIES BANK

Homophone Crossword

Prepare a crossword puzzle using **MATCHWORD**. Choose one word from each of the following pairs of homophones, and others, to list as numbered clues: *be/bee, our/hour, blue/blew, see/sea, here/hear, road/rode, cent/sent, new/knew, no/know, right/write, one/won, eight/ate*. Copy and distribute the puzzle to students. Ask them to complete the crossword puzzle by filling in each numbered item across and down with the clue word's homophone.

Meaningful Homophones

Write sets of homophones on the board, such as *here/hear, cent/sent,* and *knew/new*. Divide students into teams and give each team a different color of chalk. Then ask each team in turn questions about the meanings of specific homophones. For example: *Which word tells what you do with your ears? Which word means "in this place"?* Team members may help each other. One member of each team writes the answer on the board.

Homophone Puzzles

Write pairs of homophones on paper strips, leaving space between the words. Cut them apart with a jagged, puzzle-like cut. Make certain there are enough words for every student in class to have one. Place the words in a box and have each student pick a card. Then invite students to find their homophone partner. When everyone is matched up, have partners use their words in oral sentences while displaying their words. Use these pairs of homophones and others: *be/bee, our/hour, blue/blew, see/sea, here/hear, road/rode, cent/sent, new/knew, no/know, right/write, one/won, eight/ate.*

Spelling Homophones

Read the sentences below, one at a time. Ask students to listen for homophones. Remind them to listen for context clues to help them determine how to spell the homophone. Have students write the word on their papers.

Juan is wearing a <u>blue</u> shirt today.
Mom bought me <u>new</u> sneakers.
Do you <u>know</u> how to find the book?
I can <u>see</u> the park from my window.
This <u>road</u> has a lot of traffic!
I will <u>write</u> you a letter.
Julie scored <u>one</u> goal at today's game.
I want to <u>be</u> a teacher when I grow up.

WORD LIST

Homophones

Easy	ate/eight	hole/whole	peace/piece	their/there/they're
	be/bee	hour/our	right/write	threw/through
	blew/blue	I/eye	road/rode	to/too/two
	brake/break	its/it's	rose/rows	toe/tow
	by/buy	knew/new	sail/sale	way/weigh
	cent/sent	know/no	see/sea	weather/whether
	deer/dear	lead/led	seen/scene	weight/wait
	for/four	meet/meat	shone/shown	wood/would
	hear/here	one/won	son/sun	your/you're
Medium	bear/bare	heal/heel	plain/plane	weak/week
	berry/bury	herd/heard	so/sew	who's/whose
	do/due/dew	lie/lye	stare/stair	wrap/rap
	fare/fair	made/maid	steel/steal	
	flour/flower	mane/main	tale/tail	
	hair/hare	night/knight	toad/towed	
Hard	aloud/allowed	mail/male	principal/principle	wail/whale
	beet/beat	mantle/mantel	roll/role	waist/waste
	bread/bred	mussel/muscle	seem/seam	ware/wear
	brewed/brood	not/knot	slay/sleigh	weave/we've
	coarse/course	peak/peek	vane/vain/vein	weed/we'd
	hoarse/horse	pear/pare	wade/weighed	yoke/yolk

Circle the homophone that completes each sentence. Then write it on the line.

I am having fun _____ at camp.   hear   here

I wish you could _____ with me.   be   bee

Today I _____ a horse.   road   rode

This was a _____ skill for me.   knew   new

We learned to ride the _____ way.   right   write

My lesson lasted an _____.   hour   our

There were _____ horses on the trail.   ate   eight

My horse was the nicest _____.   one   won

I _____ I would like to ride again.   know   no

I'm happy Mom and Dad _____ me to camp!   cent   sent

Write another sentence about camp using one of these homophones: *blew, blue.*

_____

_____

_____

HOMOGRAPHS

BACKGROUND INFORMATION

Words that are spelled the same but have more than one meaning are called homographs. Although there are no differences in spelling, context clues can help students determine which meaning of a word is being used in a given sentence. If students do not know which meaning of a word is intended, suggest that they try substituting definitions for the word in the sentence. Then they can decide which meaning makes sense.

OBJECTIVES

The student will learn to
- recognize words with more than one meaning
- understand that words with the same spelling but different meanings are called homographs
- use context clues to determine the meaning of a homograph in reading
- spell some common homographs and understand the differences in meaning

PRE-CHECK

Write the following sentences on the board and read them aloud.
    Oh, no! I dropped my pen in the
    bull's pen!

Underline the words *pen* and *pen*. Call attention to the first instance of the word. Ask students what it means. Point out the second word *pen* and ask students to tell its meaning. This will give you an idea of students' awareness of homographs and their ability to use context to define them.

ELL SUPPORT

Language learners may not understand how a decoded word fits into the context of what they're reading due to their limited oral vocabularies. You can help students memorize differences in meaning by having them write a homograph, such as *bat,* and then illustrate it with two different drawings (the animal and the baseball stick). Depending on students' level of fluency and proficiency in English, you may need to show pictures to demonstrate the differences in meaning.

DEMONSTRATE

Write these sentences on the board and read them aloud:

    Rosa is <u>kind</u> to everyone.
    What <u>kind</u> of dog is that?

Say: *I see that these two sentences have a word that is spelled and pronounced the same. However, the word* kind *has a different meaning in each sentence. In the first sentence,* kind *describes something about the way Rosa treats people. What word could I substitute for* kind *in this sentence? I think it means "friendly" or "nice." I'll reread the sentence, substituting these words for* kind. *Yes, "Rosa is nice to everyone" sounds right. Now I want to find the meaning of* kind *in the next sentence. Here,* kind *seems to mean a breed of dog. The meanings "friendly" and "nice" do not make sense. What meaning does make sense? "Type" or "variety" would fit. "What type of dog is that?" makes sense. I can figure out which meaning of a word fits by using the context to guess the meaning and then substituting my definition in the sentence to check.*

Write these sentences on the board and read them aloud.

    The trunk of that tree is very slim.
    The elephant picked up a peanut with
      its trunk.
    We packed our clothes in the trunk.

Say: *I see that one word is used in all three sentences.* (Circle *trunk.) The word has a different meaning in each sentence. I am going to look the word up in the dictionary to see the different meanings it can have.*

Look up *trunk* in a dictionary and read the definitions aloud.

Say: *I see that the word* trunk *has many different meanings. They have different numbers. The word* tree *appears in one definition and also in the first sentence. "The main stem or stock of a tree" fits*

the first sentence. *The second sentence mentions the elephant, and so does the definition, "a long, flexible snout, as that of the elephant." Another definition mentions luggage and packing. The definition "a large piece of luggage used for packing and carrying clothes" makes sense for the third sentence. I know I can check meanings in the dictionary to see what meaning of a word fits in a sentence I am reading.*

COACH

Using **MATCHWORD**, create a worksheet that has sentences with homographs. After each sentence, include two or more definitions for each homograph. Read each sentence with students, then read the definitions. Ask them which meaning fits the word as it is used in the sentence. Have students circle the correct definition.

Say: *We know that some words have more than one meaning. Let's look at the context of the sentence to see what meaning makes sense. What is the first sentence? (For example, The dog sat at the foot of the stairs.) What are the definitions? (1. The end of a leg 2. The lowest part of something 3. 12 inches) Which definition makes sense for this sentence? Why do you think this? Let's substitute this definition for the word* foot *in the sentence: The dog sat at the lowest part of the stairs. This is the meaning that fits the context of the sentence.*

Continue with the other sentences on the worksheet, having students choose the meaning that fits the context.

APPLY

Use **MATCHWORD** to create games and activities that require students to identify homographs and use context to determine their meanings. For example, you might make word cards, cloze sentences, word bingo sheets, and mini sentence strips. The Activities Bank that follows provides ideas for helping students practice using homographs.

ASSESS

- Observe students as they complete the activities. Note in particular whether they can determine a homograph's meaning using context clues.
- Point to homographs on the **MATCHWORD** blackline masters students completed. Have them make up a sentence using each word with a different meaning than it had on the worksheet.
- Use the assessment blackline master provided at the end of the unit to evaluate students' understanding of homographs.

RETEACH

- Create a word wall with homographs students locate in their reading. As they add words to the wall, list the meanings of the words and have volunteers use the words in sentences.
- Present pairs of sentences that use homographs. Have students identify the homographs and pantomime or act out the meanings they have in the sentences.
- Have students write sentences for homographs that illustrate their different meanings. Encourage them to find magazine illustrations or make drawings to visually reinforce the different meanings.
- Use **MATCHWORD** to create sentences that use pairs of homographs. Next to each sentence, include one meaning for the homograph. Have students underline the word that matches the definition. For example: *I didn't feel <u>well</u> after falling into the well. (in good health)*
- Have ELL and EO students team up to cut out or draw pictures that depict homographs.

ACTIVITIES BANK

Illustrated Homograph Dictionary

Distribute clean white paper and markers. Ask students to choose a homograph from the word wall or from a list you write on the board. Have them write the word at the top of a page and then divide the page into as many sections as the word has meanings. In each section, they draw a picture illustrating one meaning of the word. Compile students' pages in alphabetical order and create a homograph dictionary. Create a heterogeneous team of ELL and EO students for this activity. ELL students will benefit from the language models.

Guess the Word

Play a guessing game in which you give meaning clues to homographs. For example, *I am thinking of a word that means "a thick mixture of flour, milk, and eggs" and "a person who uses a bat to hit a ball." What is the word?* (batter) When you are confident that students understand the game, have them think up words and clues to give classmates.

Homograph Bingo

Create, copy, and distribute to students a grid form appropriate for bingo. Provide tiles to use as markers. Write the following words on the board and have students copy them onto the grid in any order: *bat, teeth, loaf, fly, bark, ring, duck, park, saw, watch, pen, ear.* One at a time, give clues to students, such as This word means "to do little or nothing" and "the shape that bread comes in." Students then place a marker on the word *loaf.* Students say "Bingo" when they have placed three tiles in a row horizontally or vertically.

Homograph Sentence Exchange

List homographs and some of their meanings on the board. Have partners select a homograph from the list. One student writes a sentence on a paper strip using one meaning of the word and then gives the paper to his or her partner. The partner writes a sentence on the other side of the strip using another meaning of the word. Have students repeat the activity several times, taking turns going first.

Homograph Picture Match-Up

Use **MATCHWORD** to create a page that shows illustrations for two meanings of various homographs. Provide a word bank of homographs from which to choose. Have students write the homograph that fits in the blank next to the illustrations. Then have students explain the two meanings of each homograph and use them in sentences.

Dictionary Practice

Write a list of homographs such as the following on the board: *bark, batter, ring, right, block, saw, watch, bed, foot, hand.* Assign partners one of the words to look up in a dictionary. After they read the different meanings their word can have, suggest that students write a sentence using the word with each different meaning. Students can read their sentences aloud, and classmates can identify the homograph, then guess the meanings.

WORD LIST

Homographs

Easy			
ball	can	foot	row
band	close	jam	saw
bark	duck	kind	top
bat	ear	park	watch
bill	fair	pen	well
bowl	fly	ring	

Medium			
arm	crow	left	shed
bank	date	loaf	slip
batter	down	mean	spring
bear	file	palm	stick
blow	fine	pitcher	story
bore	firm	pound	tick
brush	gum	pupil	will
case	hide	rest	yard
clip	lead	school	

Hard			
air	compact	last	rose
base	dock	light	scale
bay	fast	lime	second
bluff	felt	match	squash
boil	fleet	plot	steer
boom	grave	present	stern
bow	ground	prune	tire
cape	hatch	rare	toast

Look at each picture and read the definitions next to it. In the blank, write the number of the definition that matches the picture.

_____
1 a deep, rounded dish
2 to play a game with a ball and pins

_____
1 to move a boat by using oars
2 a line of things or people

_____
1 a thing to write with
2 a place to keep animals

_____
1 furniture for sleeping
2 ground where flowers are planted

_____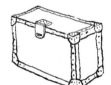
1 the main stem of a tree
2 a large box for carrying things
3 a part of an elephant

_____
1 to look at
2 a thing that tells time

_____
1 an ornament worn on the finger
2 to make a bell sound
3 a space set apart for a contest or show

_____
1 the organ of hearing in people
2 part of a plant on which grain grows

Write a sentence using the word _duck_ to mean "to stoop down quickly."

_____

_____

SECTION 3

Words with Same/ Different Meanings

ANTONYMS

BACKGROUND INFORMATION

Antonyms are words that are opposite or almost opposite in meaning, as in *on/off* and *always/never.* It is helpful to stress the word *opposite* when teaching antonyms. Consider teaching antonyms to students by using word pairs whose meanings can be readily demonstrated through concrete objects or pantomime, such as *long/short, up/down,* and *left/right.* Continue with antonyms that include high-frequency words, such as *before/after* and *under/over.* As students progress, you might introduce antonym pairs with prefixes (*tie/untie*), suffixes (*careful/careless*), and contractions (*did/didn't*).

OBJECTIVES

The student will learn to
- understand that antonyms are words with opposite meanings
- recognize antonyms
- generate and write antonyms
- spell selected pairs of antonyms

PRE-CHECK

Write the following sentence on the board and read it aloud.

My cat is happy when she can go out and sad when she has to come in.

Ask students what they can tell you about the words *happy* and *sad.* Then ask them to find other words in the sentence that are opposites. *(out/in, go/come)* Students' ability to identify these pairs and to understand opposite meanings will help you gauge their familiarity with antonyms.

ELL SUPPORT

Learning a new word along with an antonym can quicken vocabulary building. The process can be further accelerated by turning drills into fun, educational games.
- Have students make a set of illustrated flash cards with a word on one side and its opposite on the other.
- Make a set of illustrated word cards and a corresponding set of antonym cards. Mix the sets and use them for matching games.
- Write several words randomly on the board. Have two students come to the front of the room and give each a pointer. Call out the opposite of one of the words on the board. The first student to point to the correct antonym wins.

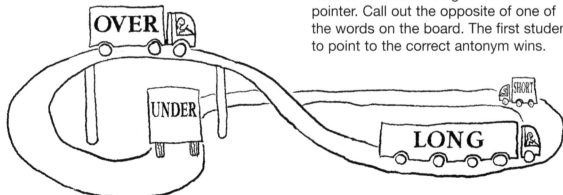

DEMONSTRATE

Use Part 1 to review the concept of antonyms and teach identification of antonyms in context. Proceed to Part 2 if you wish to teach antonym pairs with prefixes and suffixes.

PART 1

Write this sentence on the board and read it aloud.

> The picnic basket is heavy, but the blanket is light.

Say: *I see two words in this sentence that are opposites.* (Underline *heavy* and *light*.) *When I read this sentence, I think about a time when I picked up something heavy. It was hard to lift. Then I think about a time when I picked up something light. I could pick it up easily. I know that words with opposite meanings are called* antonyms. Heavy *and* light *have opposite meanings, so they are antonyms.*

Write this sentence on the board and read it aloud.

> The concrete at the pool was hot, but the water was cold.

Say: *I see two antonyms in this sentence.* (Underline *hot* and *cold*.) *I remember hot and cold things I have touched. My experience tells me that they are opposites. I remember a time when I burned my hand on a hot stove. I also remember what my hands feel like after I have been playing in the snow.* Hot *and* cold *are antonyms.*

PART 2

Write these sentences on the board and read them aloud.

> In a careless moment, Marie lost her watch. Since then, she has been more careful with her possessions.

Say: *I see two words that contain the same root word in these two sentences.* (Underline *careless* and *careful* and point out the different suffixes.) *I know that* -less *and* -ful *are suffixes. Suffixes are word parts added to words that change the meanings of those words. The suffix* -less *means "without," and the suffix* -ful *means "full of." This means that being careless means not taking care; and being careful means you do take care of things. I see that the suffixes* -less *and* -ful *can be used to make antonyms.*

Write these sentences on the board and read them aloud.

> The clerk is unable to help you now. When he finishes with this customer, he will be able to assist you.

Say: *I see two words in this sentence that are antonyms*—able *and* unable. (Circle the two words.) *I see that* unable *is made by adding the prefix* un- *to* able. *I know that the prefix* un- *means "not."* Unable *means "not able." So I know that this prefix can be added to a word to make its antonym. Do any other prefixes work in this way? I will try* dis-. *I know that* appear *and* disappear *are opposite in meaning. So are* agree *and* disagree. *I think that* dis- *also can be used to make a word's antonym.*

COACH

Using **MATCHWORD**, create a worksheet that contains sentences calling for antonyms. Place pairs of antonyms, in mixed order, in a word bank at the top of the page. Include these pairs, and others, if you wish: *long/short, always/never, up/down, left/right, laugh/cry, up/down, in/out, hot/cold, strong/weak,* *friend/enemy, fast/slow, awake/asleep, quiet/noisy.* If you have chosen to complete Part 2 as well, include antonym pairs made by adding suffixes or a prefix; for example, *careful/careless, hopeful/hopeless, happy/unhappy, like/dislike, trust/distrust.*

Say: *We need to complete these sentences by filling in the blanks with antonyms, or words that mean the opposite. Let's look for words that fit in the sentences that have opposite meanings. What is the first sentence?* (for example, *Jan loves cake and ___ orders it at a restaurant, but Joan doesn't like sweets and ___ eats them.*) *If someone loves cake, he or she would probably want to eat it a lot. I think Jan always orders it. The word* always *makes sense for the first blank. What is the opposite of* always? *Since Joan doesn't like sweet foods, she would not want to eat them.* Never *makes sense in this sentence. I will write this sentence on the board while you fill in the blanks on your paper. Did you use the same words I did? Did you spell them correctly?*

Continue with other sentences, having students fill in blanks with antonym pairs and cross the antonyms off the word bank list as they proceed.

APPLY

Use **MATCHWORD** to create games and activities that require students to identify antonyms or to generate and spell pairs of antonyms and use them in context. For example, you might make word sort columns, Go Fish cards, word bingo sheets, word searches, and crossword puzzles. The Activities Bank that follows provides ideas for helping students practice using antonyms.

ASSESS

- Observe students as they complete the activities. Note in particular whether they are able to pair words with opposite meanings and use them in context.
- Read groups of words such as these to students: *slow/lazy/fast, big/little/red, rich/poor/empty, kind/different/same.* Have them listen for and identify antonyms.
- Use the assessment blackline master provided at the end of the unit to evaluate students' understanding of antonyms.

RETEACH

- Use **MATCHWORD** to make cards for antonym pairs, one antonym on a card. Distribute the cards to students and have them find their antonym partners.
- Point out antonyms in students' reading. Have students copy the antonym pairs on index cards and put them on a word wall. Ask them to use the antonyms in sentences.
- Write antonym pairs that lend themselves to pantomime on index cards and have students draw cards, then act out the antonyms for others to guess.
- Use **MATCHWORD** to make a crossword puzzle for antonyms. Students are to think of an antonym for each clue word. You may want to provide a word box listing the antonyms students need to fill out the puzzle.

ACTIVITIES BANK

Antonym Bingo

Using **MATCHWORD**, create bingo cards with these words: *slow, open, easy, dark, cool, many, old, over, strong, happy, up, out.* Distribute the bingo cards to students. Then read the following words. Have students look for the antonyms on their bingo card and mark them with tiles or other markers: *warm, close, weak, hard, fast, few, young, light, under, sad, down, in.* Students say "Bingo!" when they have covered a row with markers either horizontally or vertically.

Describing Opposites

Group students in small groups and have them cooperate to write a descriptive paragraph about an assigned topic, such as a stormy night or a poor man. Groups then exchange paragraphs and rewrite them, replacing the descriptive words with antonyms. Invite students to read aloud both versions of paragraphs and discuss the changes in meaning.

Spelling Antonyms

Dictate each word below, one at a time. Have students repeat the word slowly and then write it. When they have written all the words, ask students to identify which pairs of words are antonyms.

| up | under | warm | slow | little |
| fast | cool | big | down | over |

Antonym Search

Use **MatchWord** to make a worksheet of antonym pairs, placing the words in random order. Duplicate the sheet and distribute copies. Pair students and have partners search for antonym pairs. They might use colored markers or highlighters to color code the antonyms on the sheet.

Color Opposites

Create an illustration that shows many pairs of opposites. Copy the illustration and give copies to students. Say pairs of sentences that direct students to identify and differentiate antonyms by color; for example, *Color the tall tree purple. Color the short tree brown.*

ACTIVITIES BANK

Find Your Opposite

Use **MATCHWORD** to make cards for words and their opposites. Place the cards in a box or bag. You may choose from these words or add others:

cold	strong	soft	open	dark	tall
thin	sweet	sell	front	finish	morning
poor	neat	dry	first	slow	heavy

Students draw cards and walk around the room showing them and looking at others' cards to find their opposites. When partners have located each other, give each pair a large sheet of paper folded in half. Each student writes his or her word on one side of the paper, illustrates its meaning, and writes a sentence using the word. Completed pages can be compiled into an antonyms book.

Animal Antonyms

On the board, write the names of animals that have opposite qualities that can be described using antonyms; for example, *cheetah/turtle (fast/slow)*, *elephant/mouse (big/small or heavy/light)*, *tiger/kitten (wild/tame)*, *giraffe/lizard (tall/short)*. Ask students to name an antonym pair that describes how the animals in each pair are different. Have them write sentences using these antonyms to compare the animals.

Opposites Attract

On strips of paper, write word groups that contain two antonyms and one unrelated word; for example, *quiet, easy, noisy; smile, chew, frown*. Pair students and have partners draw one of the strips and act out each word. Classmates can guess the words, then identify the words with opposite meanings. Write the three words on the board after each pantomime and have a volunteer circle the antonyms.

Sentence Opposites

Using **MATCHWORD**, make word cards for antonym pairs, such as *big/small, under/over, before/after,* and *lost/found*. Put each word on its own card. Place the cards for the antonym pairs side by side in a pocket chart. Ask a volunteer to read one of the words and use it in an oral sentence that shows its meaning. Then have another student use the word's antonym in a sentence. Repeat with the other words until all students have had a turn. Then mix the cards and have students sort them to remake the antonym pairs.

Name: **Date:**

Connect the antonyms in each box by drawing a line between them.

short	under
high	tall
over	enemy
friend	low

asleep	sharp
strong	up
down	weak
dull	awake

love	cool
cold	hate
joy	sorrow
warm	hot

right	buy
sell	thick
sit	stand
thin	wrong

found	lost
near	noisy
easy	far
quiet	hard

above	below
laugh	inside
outside	dark
light	cry

Write an antonym for the underlined word that would make the sentence mean the opposite.

The song made me feel <u>sad</u>.   _____

It is too <u>dark</u> in here!   _____

She has been feeling <u>well</u> today.   _____

SYNONYMS

BACKGROUND INFORMATION

Synonyms are words that have the same or nearly the same meaning, such as *cold/chilly, glad/happy*, and *quick/fast*. After students become comfortable with synonym pairs, consider presenting lists of familiar synonyms that they are likely to come across in their reading or use in their writing, for example, *large/big/huge/giant*.

Because antonyms, or words with opposite meanings, may be more obvious and more familiar to students, you may wish to teach antonyms before teaching synonyms. Then allow a period of time for students to solidify their grasp of antonyms before introducing the concept of synonyms.

OBJECTIVES

The student will learn to
- understand that synonyms are words that have the same or nearly the same meaning
- recognize synonyms
- generate and write synonyms
- spell pairs of synonyms

PRE-CHECK

Write the following sentence on the board and read it aloud.
> I'd like a big piece of cake and a large slice of pie.

Ask students to name words in the sentence that have the same, or almost the same, meaning. Their responses will give you an indication of their grasp of the concept of synonyms.

ELL SUPPORT

Learning a new word along with a synonym will accelerate vocabulary building.
1. Have students make a set of illustrated flash cards with a word on one side and a synonym on the other. Learners can use the cards to quiz themselves and each other.
2. Make a set of illustrated word cards and a matching set of synonym cards. Mix the sets and use them for matching games: Snap, Go Fish, Concentration. Keep the sets separate and organize a relay race. Runners pick up and read a word card from a pile at their feet, dash to the synonym pile, find the synonym, and bring both cards back to home base.

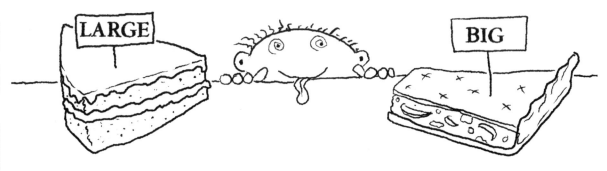

DEMONSTRATE

Write this set of sentences on the board and read them aloud.

> To run on the track team, you need to be fast. I am a fast runner. Jim is also fast.

Say: *I see that I have used the same word three times.* (Underline *fast* in each sentence.) *This makes my writing boring and less fun to read. I will substitute a* synonym, *or a word that means the same, for the word* fast *in two of the sentences. One word that means about the same as* fast *is* quick. *Another is* speedy. *I will use* quick *and* speedy *to replace the word* fast. (Cross out *fast* in sentences 2 and 3 and write *speedy* and *quick*.) *Now I'll read the sentences aloud to see if they have the same meaning.* "To run on the track team, you need to be fast. I am a speedy runner. Jim is also quick." *Yes, the meaning is the same, so I can tell that these words are synonyms.*

Write this set of words on the board and read them aloud.

> cheerful: helpful, noisy, lighthearted

Say: *I want to pick the synonym for* cheerful. *I know that* cheerful *means "full of cheer or happiness." Now I'll look at the list for a word that means the same.* Helpful *describes someone who helps. It doesn't relate to feelings.* (Cross out *helpful*.) Noisy *describes the amount of sound something or someone makes. It doesn't relate to feelings either.* (Cross out *noisy*.) Lighthearted *refers to a positive feeling; so does* cheerful. *A* lighthearted *person feels full of happiness.* Lighthearted *and* cheerful *are synonyms. To check my choice, I will try out both words in the same sentence.*

Write the following sentence on the board. Read it two times, filling in the blank each time with one of the synonyms.

> The winner had a ___ smile on her face. (cheerful/lighthearted)

Say: *Both sentences mean the same. This shows me that my choice is correct.* Cheerful *and* lighthearted *are synonyms.*

COACH

Using **MATCHWORD**, generate a worksheet with two columns of words. Be sure each word in the second column is a synonym for a word in the first column, but place them in random order. Choose from these synonym pairs and add others: *sound/noise, scared/frightened, thin/skinny, cry/weep, start/begin, sad/unhappy, close/near, gift/present, ship/boat, easy/simple.*

Say: *We need to find the words that are synonyms, or words that mean the same or almost the same. What is the first word on the list?* (for example, *easy*) *Look through the words in the second column for a word that means about the same as the word* easy. *What word do you think is a synonym for* easy?

Guide students to choose the correct synonyms for the words in the first column.

Write the following sentence on the board.

> This puzzle was ___ to do.

Say: *To check your choice, use both words in the same sentence and see if the meaning changes:* The puzzle was easy to do. The puzzle was simple to do. *Do these sentences say the same thing? Then* easy *and* simple *are synonyms.*

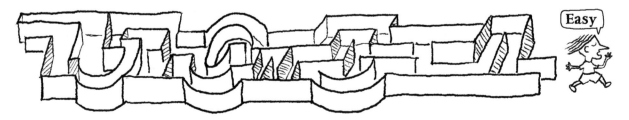

APPLY

Use **MATCHWORD** to create games and activities that require students to identify synonyms or to generate and spell pairs of synonyms and use them in context. For example, you might make word sort columns, Go Fish cards, word bingo sheets, and crossword puzzles. The Activities Bank that follows provides ideas for helping students practice using synonyms.

ASSESS

- Observe students as they complete the activities. Note in particular whether they can isolate synonyms from lists of words and can substitute synonyms for words in sentences so that meaning stays the same.
- Read groups of words such as these to students: *light/pale/dark; swift/slow/fast, woods/beach/forest, noisy/quiet/peaceful*. Have them listen for and identify synonyms.
- Use the assessment blackline master provided at the end of the unit to evaluate students' understanding of synonyms.

RETEACH

- Use **MATCHWORD** to make cards for sets of synonyms. Distribute one card to each student. Have students group themselves by finding others who have synonyms for their word.
- Have students pass a ball every time they name a synonym. Give the first student a common word; he or she names a synonym and passes the ball to the next student. Continue passing the ball until students cannot think of any more synonyms.
- Use **MATCHWORD** to create a simple story, leaving some words blank. Below each blank, write a word that fits. Read the story together, using these words. Then have students fill in the blanks with synonyms and read the story again to see if the meaning is the same.
- Make a crossword puzzle, using **MATCHWORD**. Give synonyms for puzzle words as clues. You may want to provide a word box listing the words students need to fill in the puzzle.

ACTIVITIES BANK

Synonym Concentration

Using **MATCHWORD**, prepare sets of cards for synonyms (for example, *junk/trash, little/tiny, close/shut, sick/ill, noise/sound, quick/fast, road/street, shout/yell*). Let pairs of students use the cards to play Concentration. Players alternate turning over two cards at a time, trying to match words with the same meaning. The cards can also be used to play a version of Go Fish. Have ELL students look through magazines and cut out pictures for the synonyms to add to the word cards. They can scramble the cards and match up the synonym pairs.

Synonym Match

Make large word cards for pairs of synonyms, writing one word on the left side of a card and its synonym on the right, with space between the words. Cut all the cards into halves. Display one set of card halves on a bulletin board or other surface and place the other set of halves in a basket, box, or bag. Have students pick a card half and place the word next to its synonym, then use the synonyms in a sentence.

Synonym Search

Use **MATCHWORD** to make a worksheet of synonym pairs or sets, placing the words in random order. Duplicate and distribute the sheet. Have students use markers or highlighters of different colors to color-code the synonym sets, then write them on another paper. Ask students to write a sentence that calls for one of their synonyms, leaving the space blank. As students read their sentences aloud, classmates can search their sheets of synonyms to select the set that could be used to fill in the blank.

Clue Me In

Introduce students to a game in which a player asks questions that can be answered with a synonym; for example, "What is a synonym for *ship* that rhymes with *goat?*" (boat) "What is a synonym for *angry* that has only three letters?" (mad) Challenge students to write several questions. They can exchange papers and write the answers to each other's questions.

Ad Specialist

Have students choose an advertisement from a flyer, newspaper, or magazine. They are to rewrite the ad by substituting synonyms for words in the ad. Have students read aloud the original ads and their rewrites. Discuss any differences in meaning that may have been caused by the changes.

ACTIVITIES BANK

Synonym Web

Make a word web on the board. Draw a center circle with outer circles connected to it by lines, as in the sample below. Write a word such as *fast* in the center circle. Ask students to think of as many words as they can that have the same or almost the same meaning as *fast*. Let volunteers write those words in the outer circles of the web. Add circles and lines as needed. Encourage students to look for synonyms in dictionaries and thesauruses if they wish.

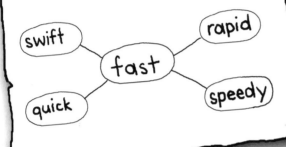

Spelling Synonyms

Dictate each word below, in random order, one at a time. Suggest that students repeat the word to themselves, identify the sounds, and write the letters that stand for those sounds. After students have written all the words, ask them to tell which pairs of words are synonyms.

fix/mend   little/tiny   huge/large
unhappy/sad   creep/crawl   well/healthy

Class Thesaurus

Divide students into small groups. Assign each group a common word (such as *small*, *large*, *good*, *bad*, *cold*, *hot*, *happy*, *sad*, *fat*, *thin*). Have students brainstorm a list of synonyms. Encourage them to name all the words they can and put them into these categories: "Exact Synonyms," "Words with Similar Meanings." Have students write their entry word at the top of a sheet of paper, then their lists of both categories of synonyms. Invite groups to continue, using other words you assign. Organize students' pages alphabetically and make a class thesaurus.

Find the Mates

Create a number of word groups that contain two synonyms, such as the following and others: *funny, joke, amusing, sad; choose, select, ticket, refuse; farming, plow, crops, agriculture.* Divide students into two teams. Read a group of words to one team and have them identify the synonyms in the group. If they are unable to select the synonyms, play passes to the second team. Give one point for each successful pairing of synonyms. Try to begin with simpler lists and work toward more difficult words.

Connect the synonyms in each box by drawing a line between them.

glad	mad
unhappy	close
near	happy
angry	sad

easy	damp
giggle	present
gift	simple
wet	laugh

scared	big
pal	friend
small	afraid
large	tiny

thin	weep
cry	great
good	bad
naughty	skinny

sound	enjoy
quick	fast
sick	noise
like	ill

smile	crawl
creep	boat
ship	begin
start	grin

Write a synonym to replace the word in parentheses in each sentence.

The sidewalk was _____ (hot) to my bare feet.

Mark is _____ (sick) and cannot go to school today.

Good for you! That answer is _____ (correct).

Shortened Words

CONTRACTIONS

BACKGROUND INFORMATION

A contraction is a short way of writing two or more words. The words are put together, with an apostrophe taking the place of one or more letters that are left out. Students need to understand that

- most contractions are made of a verb plus *not (should not/shouldn't, cannot/can't)* or of a pronoun plus a verb *(I have/I've, that is/that's)*
- sometimes the spelling changes when the contraction is formed *(will not/won't)*, and sometimes the vowel sound changes *(do not, don't)*.
- there are other types of contractions, such as *o'clock* for *of the clock, let's* for *let us*, and a noun plus a verb *(Rob is/Rob's)*.
- contractions are used informally, most often in story dialogue

It is important for students to recognize the difference between possessives and contractions.

OBJECTIVES

The student will learn to
- recognize, read, and form contractions
- use structural analysis to identify the words that form a contraction
- spell some common contractions

PRE-CHECK

Write the following sentences on the board, underlined as shown, and read them aloud.

I'm so excited. I haven't been here before!

Invite students to tell you what is the same about the words *I'm* and *haven't*. Ask them what two words were put together to form the contractions and what letters were left out. Use students' responses to assess their familiarity with contractions.

ELL SUPPORT

Official contractions don't exist in most languages, and some learners feel that these forms are incorrect or lazy.

Major pronunciation problems:
- **I'm:** *I'm* = /in/ or /ing/
- **can't, don't:** *can't* = can; *don't* = /dunt/
- **'ll:** Learners drop /l/ or change it to /ər/.
- **wouldn't, couldn't, shouldn't:** Students pronounce the silent *l;* change /o͝o/ to /o͞o/; drop /n/, /t/, or /nt/; or overpronounce /dn/.
- **let's:** *-t's* is a difficult consonant cluster. Students may drop one or both sounds. They may also pronounce /l/ as /r/ or /n/.

I shouldn't have eaten that contraction.

DEMONSTRATE

The Demonstrate section of the lesson is divided into two parts. Part 1 shows students how to analyze the structure of contractions and identify the words used to form them. Part 2 should help students who are having difficulty writing contractions by looking at how to form contractions. You may choose to use only Part 1, only Part 2, or both.

PART 1

Write the following sentence on the board, underlining the contraction, and read it aloud.

You're my best friend.

Say: *I see that this sentence has a contraction. A contraction is a short form of two words. One or more letters are replaced with an apostrophe.* (Circle the apostrophe with colored chalk.) *When I look at the contraction* you're, *I first see the word* you. (Bracket *you*.) *The second word must be a word that ends in* -re. (Bracket the *'re* portion.) *One or more letters are missing because they have been replaced by the apostrophe. The word* are *would make sense in this sentence. I think* a *has been replaced by the apostrophe.* You're *is the short form for* you are. (Write *you are* above the contraction.)

Add this sentence on the board and read it aloud, underlining the contraction.

I won't tell anyone the secret.

Say: *The contraction* won't *is made by putting together* not *and another word. I know that* n't *stands for* not. (Bracket *n't*.) *The* o *has been replaced by an apostrophe.* (Circle the apostrophe with colored chalk, then write *not* above *n't*.) *The rest of the contraction is not a word I recognize.* (Bracket *wo*.) *I think the spelling of this word was changed to form the contraction. I'll look at the context of the sentence to see what word would make sense in this place.* (Read *I __ not tell anyone the secret.*) *The word*

will *or* would *makes sense. But I know that* wouldn't *is the contraction for* would not. *So this contraction must stand for* will not. *I think the spelling was changed because* willn't *is too hard to say. The letters* -ill *are replaced by* o.

PART 2

Write the following word equation on the board:

I + will = Iwill = I'll

Say: *This equation shows me how to form the contraction* I'll *from the words* I will. *First, I put* I *and* will *together.* (Underline *I* and *will*, then *Iwill* as you say this.) *Now, to shorten the second word, I'll cross out the* w *and* i. (Cross out *wi*.) *Then I'll add an apostrophe where the letters were.* (Write an apostrophe over the slash.) *The finished contraction looks like this.* (Circle *I'll*.)

Continue with other examples, such as *does + not, could + have,* and *that + is.*

COACH

Using **MATCHWORD**, create a worksheet with this list of contractions, followed by blank lines: *couldn't, it's, aren't, would've, I'm, won't, didn't, can't, you've, he'll, we'll, they're.* Below the list, provide a word bank of the pairs of words used to make these contractions, in random order.

Say: *How do we tell what two words were used to form a contraction? We know that one of the words is left whole and that one or more letters are left out of the other word and replaced by an apostrophe. Let's look at the first contraction on the worksheet.* (for example, *couldn't*) *What word do we recognize in the first part of the contraction? That's right. We see the word* could. *The second part is* n-apostrophe-t. *We know the apostrophe takes the place of a letter or letters. What letter could we put with* n *and* t *to make a word? The letter* o *would make the word* not, *then the phrase would be* could not. *Let's look at the word bank. Is could not there? Yes, it is. I'll write this phrase on the board. You write it on the blank on your paper. Did you write the words correctly? Check to see that they are spelled right.*

After you and the students have completed Part 2 of the Demonstrate section of the lesson, use **MATCHWORD** to create a worksheet listing word pairs that can be used to form contractions, with a blank after each pair. Ask students how they would change each pair to form a contraction. Have them write the contracted form in the blank.

Say: *What is the first pair of words on this page?* (for example, *should have*) *We know that to form a contraction, we first put the two words together.* (Write *shouldhave* on the board.) *Next, we take out one or more letters and replace them with an apostrophe. Which letters should we cross out? That's right; we'll cross out the vowel.* (Cross out *a*. Add an apostrophe above it.) *This leaves* shouldh've*. That doesn't look right, does it? That's too hard to pronounce. Let's cross out the* h *too.* (Cross out the *h*.) Should've *sounds familiar. Now I'll write the contraction on the board while you write it on your paper. Compare what you wrote with what I wrote.*

Have ELL students work with an EO student to complete the exercises.

APPLY

Use **MATCHWORD** to create games and activities that require students to identify contractions or to generate and spell contractions. For example, you might make word sort columns, Go Fish cards, Word Bingo sheets, and crossword puzzles. The Activities Bank that follows provides ideas for helping students practice using contractions.

ASSESS

- Observe students as they complete the activities. Note in particular whether they can identify the words used to form a contraction and recognize what letters have been omitted.
- Read words to students slowly, one at a time: *haven't, has, should've, good, well, we'll, don't, couldn't, hat, I've, what's*, etc. Ask students to raise their hands when they hear a contraction. Have volunteers write the contractions on the board, read them, and tell what two words are used to form them.
- Use the assessment blackline master provided at the end of the unit to evaluate students' understanding of contractions.

RETEACH

- Write sentences on the board, underlining words that can be contracted. Read each sentence aloud and invite students to read it, substituting the contraction. Have students direct you to cross out the words and spell the contraction above them.
- Model forming contractions using equations such as this on the board: *do + not = donot − o + ' = don't.* Have students form contractions using such equations until they are able to leave out the middle portion.
- Have students locate contractions in their reading. Write each contraction on chart paper. Work with students to spell out the words used to form it, using a reasoning process such as this: *1. Contraction:* could've, *2. Made up of:* could + __ve, *3. What second word might be:* have, love, give, *4. Substitute word for apostrophe and letters in sentence:* could have *makes sense*
- Use **MATCHWORD** to make a crossword puzzle, giving contractions as clue words. Students complete the puzzle by spelling out the words used to form the contractions.
- Post a contraction chart in clear view. When students find contractions in their reading, have them refer to the chart to see what words have been used to form the contractions.

ACTIVITIES BANK

Contraction Match-Up

Using **MATCHWORD**, make pairs of word cards with a contraction on one and the words used to form the contraction on the other. Pin each set on a bulletin board in a column in random order. Invite small groups of students to rearrange the word pairs in the second column to match their contractions. Have students read aloud the paired cards and use the contractions in sentences to prove they have matched them correctly.

Contraction Categories Chart

Have students work with partners to find contractions in books they are reading. To avoid confusion of possessives and contractions, encourage them to reread the sentence, replacing the word with an apostrophe with the two words they think form it. If the sentence makes sense, the word is a contraction. Have students create a contraction chart with categories such as "Contractions with *not*," "Contractions with *are*," and so on. Students can list contractions in one column and the two words used to form them in a second column.

Contraction Equations

Use **MATCHWORD** to prepare a worksheet of contraction equations. Possibilities include the following:

will + not = ___, let + us = ___, she + has = ___, we + had = ___, I + have = ___, you + are = ___, have + not = ___.

Provide letter cards and apostrophe cards (or elbow macaroni). Students can use the cards to form contractions that solve the equations.

The Play's the Thing

Write a simple dialogue using no contractions, such as the one below. Duplicate the lines and distribute them to pairs of students. Ask students to find words that could be changed to contractions and rewrite the dialogue on the right-hand side of the page substituting the contractions. Have partners read the dialogue with contractions and without to see which one sounds more natural.

Speaker 1: *Where did you go?*
Speaker 2: *I have been at the mall.*
Speaker 1: *Hey! I would have gone with you.*
Speaker 2: *I did not know I was going until the last second.*
Speaker 1: *Now I will not get to spend my birthday money.*

Contraction Concentration

Using **MATCHWORD**, prepare word cards for an assortment of words that can be contracted and matching cards with the contractions. Have pairs or groups of students use the cards to play Concentration, trying to match words and contractions. The cards could also be used to play Go Fish.

Fluency Practice

Have students make word cards, writing a contraction on one side and the two words used to form the contraction on the other side. Pair students to use the cards as flash cards to practice identifying the words used to form contractions.

**Find the contraction in the box
for each pair of words below.
Write the contraction on the line.**

I am trying to find
the contractions and
I will not give up!

| it's | aren't | would've | won't |
| they're | you've | he'll | I'm |

would have _____   they are _____

are not _____   it is _____

will not _____   you have _____

he will _____   I am _____

**Write the words used to make each contraction
on the first line. Write the letters that are left out
to make the contraction on the second line.**

Ha ha!
Left out
letters!

Contraction	Two Words	Letters Left Out
haven't	_____	_____
shouldn't	_____	_____
we'll	_____	_____
could've	_____	_____
that's	_____	_____
he'll	_____	_____
we're	_____	_____

ABBREVIATIONS

BACKGROUND INFORMATION

An abbreviation is a shortened form of a written word or phrase used in place of the whole. Students need to know that

- when abbreviations are read aloud, many are spoken as if the word were spelled out.
- abbreviations for titles *(Mr., Dr., Gen.)*, days *(Mon.),* and months *(Sept.)* are capitalized and end with a period.
- abbreviations of some organizations and government agencies are formed from the initial letters of the complete name *(FBI, NASA).* These are called acronyms.
- acronyms may be pronounced as though they are words themselves, or their letters may be spelled out. Rarely (as in *CD-ROM*), both methods are used together.
- acronyms and two-letter postal abbreviations for the 50 states *(AZ, VA)* are all capital letters and are not followed by periods.
- abbreviations for titles are acceptable in both ordinary and formal writing, but most other abbreviations are not.

OBJECTIVES

The student will learn to
- recognize, read, and form abbreviations
- capitalize and punctuate abbreviations correctly
- spell abbreviations

PRE-CHECK

Write the following sentence on the board and read it aloud.

Mr. and Mrs. Morse live at 12 Oak St. in Taos, NM.

Invite students to tell you what they notice about several of the words in the sentence. Have them underline the abbreviations and tell what they represent. Use students' responses to assess their familiarity with abbreviations and the conventions of capitalizing and punctuating abbreviations.

ELL SUPPORT

Abbreviations are deceptive for most speakers of English as a second language.
- Each letter can be pronounced separately: *P.M., A.M.* Some learners may group letters into words: *a.m.* = am; *UFO* = /yo͞ofō/.
- An abbreviation can be pronounced as a word *(scuba* = /skü bə/) or as a mixture of letters and "words": *CD-ROM* = /sē dē rom/.

Some abbreviations are written forms that must be "stretched" into words. The individual letters must not be pronounced separately: *Mr.* = /mistər/; *Ms.* = /miz/, *Mrs.* = /misiz/. In these examples, students often substitute /e/ for /i/ or fail to make the /z/ in *Ms.*: *Ms. = Miss.*

DEMONSTRATE

The Demonstrate section of the lesson is divided into two parts. Part 1 focuses on abbreviations that call for initial capital letters and ending periods: titles, days of the week, months, and place name abbreviations. Part 2 addresses abbreviations spelled with all capital letters and without periods. You may choose to use only Part 1, only Part 2, or both parts.

PART 1

Write the following sentence on the board, underlining the abbreviations, and read it aloud.

You can see <u>Dr.</u> Menendez <u>Thurs.</u>, <u>Jan.</u> 23, at 2 <u>P.M.</u>

Say: *I see four words that have been abbreviated in this sentence. I know that an abbreviation is a shortened form of a word. Each of these abbreviations has one or two periods. This helps me to know that the word has been shortened.* Dr. *stands for* doctor, Thurs. *stands for* Thursday; Jan. *stands for* January; *and* P.M. *stands for* post meridian, *which means "afternoon."* (Write the word(s) for each abbreviation on the board and draw an arrow from the word(s) to the abbreviation.) *Why are the first three abbreviations capitalized? Proper nouns such as a person's name are always capitalized.*

The title used with the name is also capitalized. Days of the week and months of the year are also proper nouns, so their abbreviations are capitalized, too. When I read these abbreviations, I know I should say the word as though it were spelled out. For A.M. *and* P.M., *we just say the letters, because they are used often and stand for a Latin phrase not many people know.*

Continue, adding other title, month, and day abbreviations and modeling their full spelling.

Add this address to the board and read it aloud, underlining the abbreviation.

300 <u>E.</u> Hillcrest <u>Ave.</u>, <u>Apt.</u> 101A, Aurora, IL

Say: *This is an address. I know that when you write an address, you can use abbreviations to save space.* E. *stands for* East; Ave. *stands for* Avenue, *and* Apt. *stands for* Apartment. (Write the word for each abbreviation on the board and connect each word to its abbreviation with an arrow.) *These abbreviations are also capitalized because they are proper nouns; they name particular places. When I read these abbreviations, I also say the whole word as though it had been spelled out.*

Continue, adding other place name abbreviations (such as *St., Blvd., Pl., W.*) and modeling their full spellings.

PART 2

List the following acronyms and state abbreviations on the board.

NASA   AL
FBI   AR

Say: *These abbreviations look different. They are formed from all capital letters and they do not have any periods. The abbreviations in the first column are made from the initials of the full name of an organization or business. I know that* NASA *stands for* National Aeronautics and Space Administration; FBI *stands for* Federal Bureau of Investigation. (Write these words as you say them and underline the first letter of each word.) *When I read this type of abbreviation, I say the letters or I say the abbreviation as a word. This is because we shorten these names to make them easier.* (Circle *AL* and *AR*.) *I have seen these abbreviations on envelopes. They stand for the state names* Alabama *and* Arkansas. *I know that the U.S. Postal Service uses two-letter abbreviations, like these, for the 50 states. I should use the abbreviations with no periods when I write addresses for letters and envelopes.*

COACH

Using **MATCHWORD**, generate a worksheet with abbreviations for days of the week, months of the year, titles, such as *Dr., Mr., Ms., Gen.*, and *Rev.*, and place names such as *St., Blvd., Ave.*, and *Pl.* Next to each abbreviation, place a row of blanks that matches the number of letters in the word. Below the list, provide a word bank of the words for which these abbreviations stand, in random order. Ask students to identify the word for which each abbreviation stands and to write it next to the abbreviation.

Say: *How can we tell what word an abbreviation stands for? Let's look at the first abbreviation.* (for example, *Ave.*) *These three letters are part of a longer word. We can see that this word has six letters by counting the number of blanks. Let's look at the words in*

the word bank. *Which one begins with* a-v-e? *Does it have six letters? Do we think that* Ave. *is the abbreviation for* Avenue? *OK, let's write* avenue *on the worksheet.*

Continue with other abbreviations on the list.

After you and the students have completed Part 2 of the Demonstrate section of the lesson, use **MATCHWORD** to create a worksheet of names of organizations whose abbreviations are formed from initial letters (for example, *American Broadcasting Company, Internal Revenue Service, Home Box Office*) and the names of states (for example, *Massachusetts, Colorado, Indiana, Washington, Rhode Island*). Place a blank line to the right of each name. Below the list, provide a word bank of abbreviations from which students can choose. Ask them to write an abbreviation for each name and explain why they chose each one.

Say: *These abbreviations are those that are formed from the initial letters of the names of organizations and of states. Let's look at the list of organizations on the worksheet. What is the first organization named on the list?* (for example, *Home Box Office*) *What are the initial letters of* Home Box Office? *OK, write the abbreviation for* Home Box Office *on the worksheet. I'll write it on the board. Did you write it on your worksheet the same way that I wrote it on the board? Did you use all capital letters and no periods?*

Continue with other abbreviations of organizations and states on the list.

APPLY

Use **MATCHWORD** to create games and activities that require students to identify abbreviations or to abbreviate words and phrases and spell abbreviations. For example, you might make word sort columns, Go Fish cards, Word Pages, and mini-sentence strips. The Activities Bank that follows provides ideas for helping students practice using abbreviations. (Note: Where appropriate, pair or group ELL students with varying proficiency levels in English. ELL students benefit from good English-speaking role models.)

ASSESS

- Observe students as they complete the activities. Note in particular whether they can identify the words for abbreviations and know when to use periods and capital letters in writing abbreviations.
- Write the sentences below on the board, as shown. Read each sentence aloud and ask students to tell you which word is an abbreviation and how to write it correctly.
    In nov I'll be ten years old.
    I saw dr Davis when I was sick.
    Last thurs I went shopping on Beech ave in Charleston, S.C.
- Use the assessment blackline master provided at the end of the unit to evaluate students' understanding of abbreviations.

RETEACH

- Ask students to name adults they know in school and their neighborhoods. Write the names on the board as they are offered, using abbreviations for titles. Have students underline the periods and capital letters. Review that titles can be abbreviated when they are used with names, and they are always capitalized because the names are capitalized.
- Have students refer to a calendar to name the months of the year and days of the week. Write the full names on the board and their abbreviations next to them. (Note that *May, June,* and *July* are not abbreviated.) Have volunteers spell each abbreviation, taking care to include capitals and periods. Provide calendar forms on which students can write these abbreviations.
- As you teach state names, model the U.S. Postal Service abbreviation for each. Review the use of other place name abbreviations, such as *St., Ave.,* and *Blvd.* Give students envelopes on which to practice writing addresses (for example, of friends or relatives) with abbreviations.

ACTIVITIES BANK

Abbreviation Concentration

Using **MATCHWORD**, prepare game cards for Concentration by making one set of cards with the full names and another set of cards with their abbreviations. Use names of months, days of the week, and states, titles, place names, and other abbreviations you want students to learn. Mix the cards and place them face down. Players turn over two cards at a time, trying to match a word and its abbreviation.

Partner Practice

Provide partners with lists that include titles, names of days, months, and states, and so on. Partners take turns reading aloud the words on their list and spelling the abbreviations. Model correct spelling to indicate any capital letter and period; for example, "Capital *A-p-r*-period" (Apr.) or "Capital *C*-Capital *A*" (CA).

Titled People

Encourage students to find and bring in examples of abbreviated titles for people in newspapers, magazines, stories, and books. Set up a bulletin board or word wall of abbreviations for the titles they find. Help students determine the words for which the abbreviations stand.

Measurement Abbreviation Challenge

Ask students to look through math and science texts to find examples of abbreviations used in describing measured quantities. Have students make a chart listing the abbreviations paired with the words they abbreviate. Invite students to explain reasons why some abbreviations are capitalized and some are not, or why some use periods and some do not (for example, *in., tsp., cm, F*).

Abbreviation Relay

Write abbreviations and words that can be abbreviated, such as those below, on the board in two columns. Form two teams and have students in each team line up as they would to run a relay race. When you say "Go," the first person in line on each team goes to the board, chooses a word or an abbreviation from the team's list, and writes either the word's abbreviation or the word for the abbreviation. This "runner" then tags the next player, who repeats the procedure. Continue until all words and abbreviations have been converted. Together, check answers and have volunteers make corrections.

Team 1		Team 2	
Sunday	_____	Kentucky	_____
Mar.	_____	August	_____
Doctor	_____	Mr.	_____
September	_____	Jan.	_____
St.	_____	Apartment	_____
Minnesota	_____	Thurs.	_____

State Rhymes

To help students learn the two-letter U.S. Postal Service abbreviations for the states, have them make up two-line rhymes using state names (for example, *Maine/brain, Kentucky/lucky, Arkansas/draw*). When they write their rhymes, students are to use the state abbreviation (for example, *Dan'l Boone was feeling lucky/he'd wandered into old KY*). Post the rhymes around the room and give students time to read each other's rhymes and identify the abbreviated state names.

Choose the word from the box that matches each abbreviation. Write it on the line.

Abbreviations make my nose last longer.

October	Monday	August
Colorado	Doctor	Mister
Tuesday	Friday	General
March	Alaska	Wednesday
New Mexico	Saturday	Michigan

Sat. _____ Fri. _____

Mar. _____ Mr. _____

Dr. _____ AK _____

NM _____ Aug. _____

Oct. _____ CO _____

Gen. _____ Wed. _____

Tues. _____ Mon. _____

MI _____

Write the abbreviation for each underlined word on the line.

970 Pine Hill <u>Road</u> _____

<u>Apartment</u> 106A _____

Conway, <u>Massachusetts</u> 01341 _____

<u>January</u> 4 _____

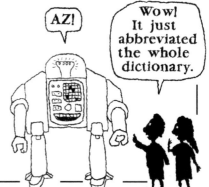

AZ!

Wow! It just abbreviated the whole dictionary.

Capitalization

CAPITALIZATION

BACKGROUND INFORMATION

Capital letters are used for several different reasons. Students need to understand that

- capital letters signal the beginning of sentences
- a capital letter is always used for the pronoun *I*
- capital letters are used at the beginning of proper nouns, proper adjectives, days of the week, months of the year, and titles of people
- capital letters are used for the first word and all important words in the titles of books, stories, poems, songs, and movies

OBJECTIVES

The student will learn to

- understand why certain words begin with capital letters
- capitalize names of places, days, months, and holidays
- capitalize the first word and all important words in titles

PRE-CHECK

Write the following sentence on the board and read it aloud.

she said i am seeing dr. kane on tuesday, october 12.

Ask students to tell you which words in the sentence should begin with capital letters. Have volunteers change the letters to capitals. Note which uses of capitalization students readily recognize and which, if any, they do not. This will help you know which uses of capitalization students need to work on.

ELL SUPPORT

Some languages capitalize words that English does not capitalize; some use lowercase letters where English uses capitals. Still others have no uppercase letters at all. In many languages, capital letters are not used for names of places, days, or months. For example, names of the days and months are not capitalized in Spanish. Book titles can be confusing for all learners, because in English titles some words are capitalized, and others—articles, conjunctions, and prepositions—are not. You can help students recognize titles by pointing out that they are indicated by quotation marks, underlines, or italics.

DEMONSTRATE

The Demonstrate section of the lesson is divided into three parts. Some students may consistently use capital letters at the beginning of sentences and for the pronoun *I*. For these students, move on to Parts 2 and 3. Depending on ELL students' level of English proficiency, you may need to demonstrate one sentence example at a time.

PART 1

Write these sentences on the board.
   Many books were on the shelves.
   The librarian said I could look for the one
      I wanted.

Say: *Most of the letters I use in a sentence are lowercase. But I capitalize some letters to signal specific things. In the first sentence, only the first letter of the first word is capitalized. I always capitalize the first letter of the first word of a sentence. In the second sentence, the first letter of the first word is capitalized. The pronoun I is also capitalized. I always capitalize the pronoun* I.

PART 2

Write these sentences on the board.
   Today is Tuesday, September 21.
   Tonight is the beginning of Rosh
      Hashanah, the Jewish New Year.
   Did you know that Leon is visiting
      from Mexico City?

Say: *I capitalized the first letter of the first word in each sentence. I also capitalized several other words. I did that because proper nouns and proper adjectives are always capitalized. In the first sentence, I capitalized the words* Tuesday *and* September. *Why? Because the names of the days of the week and the months of the year are proper nouns. They name particular things. In the second sentence, I capitalized* Rosh Hashanah *and* New Year. *They also name particular things—holidays.* Jewish *is a proper adjective, so I capitalized it. In the last sentence, I capitalized* Leon. *It is a proper noun. It names a particular person. I also capitalized* Mexico City. *It is a proper noun. It names a particular place.*

PART 3

Write these sentences on the board.
   Josh and Ms. Perkins saw Dr. Jackson
      at the mall.
   We will read the story "Borreguita and
      the Coyote" by Verna Aardema.

Say: *The first sentence has the names of three people. I capitalized each name. I also capitalized the titles* Ms. *and* Dr. *Titles that come before a person's name, like these and* Mr. *and* Mrs., *are also capitalized. In the second sentence, I capitalized the proper noun. I also capitalized the story title. When I write the title of a book, story, play, or movie, I capitalize the main words. I don't capitalize* and *or* the *unless it comes at the beginning of the title. I also don't capitalize words like* of, for, *and* in. *Notice that these are short words that are not important to the meaning of the title. I can tell that "Borreguita and the Coyote" is a story title because it has quotation marks around it. Book titles are underlined or printed in italics.*

COACH

Using **MATCHWORD**, create word cards that, when combined, will make several sentences. Display the cards on a table. Have students come to the table in pairs or small groups. Ask them to arrange words into a sentence and to write their sentence on the board. Pair ELL students with a limited level of English proficiency with English Only speakers.

Say: *Let's see how we can make a sentence using these words. We might begin with a noun:* cat. *Oh, but we'll need a* the *in front of the noun:* the cat. *Now let's pick a verb:* ran. *And a word to finish the sentence:* home. The cat ran home. *Now let's write our sentence on the board. What do we need to remember about writing a sentence? That's right; always capitalize the first word.*

Next, use **MATCHWORD** to create a list of cloze sentences that must be completed with a proper noun or a proper adjective. For example, "My favorite holiday is _____." "My next-door neighbor is _____."

Say: *Let's complete the first sentence together.* (for example, *My birthday is _____.*) *To complete this sentence, we each need to write the month, date, and year of our birthday. What do we need to remember when we write the name of the month? That's right; the name of the month always begins with a capital letter. As we complete the other sentences, we'll be sure to use capital letters for proper nouns and adjectives, titles, and the pronoun* I.

Have volunteers write the words they used to complete the sentences on the board. After they have written their words, have them explain why they capitalized particular words.

GAMES

APPLY

Use **MATCHWORD** to create games and activities that encourage students to use capitalization correctly. These might include sentence strips, cloze sentences, and journals. The Activities Bank that follows provides ideas for helping students practice using capitalization.

ASSESS

- Observe students as they complete the activities.
- Listen as students explain to the class reasons for using capital letters on their **MATCHWORD** blackline masters.
- Use the assessment blackline master provided at the end of the unit to evaluate students' understanding of capitalization.

RETEACH

- Use **MATCHWORD** to create sheets of sentences with no capital letters. Have students provide correct capitalization.
- Choose several books from the classroom bookshelves. Show the books, one at a time, and ask students to tell which words are capitalized in the title and why.
- Display a calendar. Discuss with students the words that are capitalized on it: names of months, days of the week, and holidays.
- Have students list the names of their classmates. Discuss using capital letters at the beginning of both first and last names.
- Pair ELL students with English Only students. Have them cut out magazine captions and articles and discuss what words are capitalized and why.

ACTIVITIES BANK

Book Journal

Have students create a journal of books they have read. Each page should tell the title of the book, its author, its setting, and its main characters. Students may also write a brief critique of the book. Remind them that book titles are underlined. Display pages in the journals and discuss which words are capitalized and why.

Neighborhood Maps

Have students draw and label a map of a part of their neighborhood that has stores, schools, and other buildings and places. Ask them to label the streets and landmarks on the map, using capital letters correctly. Display the maps.

Sentence Correction

Using **MATCHWORD**, make sentence strips in which capital letters are omitted. Have students choose a strip and rewrite the sentence on a sheet of paper, using capital letters correctly. Use sentences like these.

thanksgiving is on a thursday in november.
did you watch sesame street when you were younger?
a book i loved was treasure island.
we are going with mr. and mrs. aguilera to mexico city next april.

You may wish to use an overhead projector to make this activity guided practice for ELL students. Write the sentences on a transparency and discuss them with students. Then have students take turns making corrections and discussing them.

Autobiography

Have students write books about themselves. Encourage them to create pages that describe places they have lived; their birthdate; their favorite books, movies, and television programs; their favorite kinds of food; and their favorite holidays. Have students exchange books with a partner and check for correct capitalization.

Sentence Dictation

Have each student write a sentence that mentions days, months, places, holidays, people, or book titles. As students read their sentences aloud, the rest of the class can write the sentence, using capital letters where necessary.

Food Sentences

Use **MATCHWORD** to create word cards for words that name foods from various countries, such as tacos, hamburgers, spaghetti, pizza, hot dogs, chow mein, and sushi. Have small groups of students draw several cards and write sentences describing the food's nationality. For example, "Tacos are a Mexican food." Students may enjoy discussing the origins of the foods. Point out that certain foods may have originated in a particular country and then become universal.

Read the paragraph. Cross out words that need to be capitalized. Write the words correctly on the line above.

Today we started on our vacation to colorado! our whole family flew

on national Airlines to the town of fort collins. Liz, mike, and i took

turns sitting by the window so we could see out. when I wasn't

looking out, I read my book, *my side of the mountain*. All at once, i

saw tall, snow-covered mountains. dad said those were the rocky

mountains. our friend harry clark was there to meet our plane. We

will stay with him at 2413 briar lane until saturday. Then we will

drive to rocky mountain national park to camp. cool! Tonight we are

going to watch one of my favorite movies, *jurassic park*. i think this

will be the best vacation yet!

Permission is given to instructors to reproduce this page for classroom use with *Fast Track Reading*. Copyright ©2002 Wright Group/McGraw-Hill

SECTION 6

Dictionary Skills

DICTIONARY SKILLS

BACKGROUND INFORMATION

A dictionary is a reference book that gives many kinds of useful information about words. Students need to understand that

- entry words in a dictionary are arranged in alphabetical order
- an entry word may be divided into syllables by dots or spaces
- the pronunciation is given in parentheses following the entry
- symbols used to indicate pronunciation are explained in a pronunciation key
- abbreviations are given for the part of speech, followed by the definition(s) of the word
- guide words indicate the first and last entry words found on that page

OBJECTIVES

The student will learn to
- alphabetize words to the second letter
- use guide words to locate words in the dictionary
- determine the part of speech of entry words
- use words found in a dictionary in a sentence

PRE-CHECK

Write the word *loyal* on the board. Ask students what book they could use to find out the meaning of the word. Ask them what other information about the word they could find in that book. Then write the word *lunar* on the board. Ask students whether they would find the word *loyal* before or after *lunar* in the dictionary. Then write the word *litter* and have students tell whether *loyal* would be found before or after it. Their answers will help you determine how much students know about the information found in the dictionary and how to find a word in the dictionary.

ELL SUPPORT

Learners coming from a different language, especially from a language using a Roman alphabet with letters different from English, may be at a disadvantage learning alphabetical order. These students may also be unused to books that open from right to left and to reading from left to right and from top to bottom. This can make recognizing guide words difficult and locating words frustrating.

DEMONSTRATE

The Demonstrate section of the lesson is divided into two parts. Some students may already be proficient in alphabetizing words and finding words in the dictionary. For these students, move on to Part 2.

PART 1

Hold up a dictionary.

Say: *I know that I can find out many things about words in a dictionary. But first I have to know how to find words in it.*

Write these words on the board.
   sly
   carriage
   gentle
   wealth
   modern

Say: *I know that words are arranged in a dictionary in alphabetical, or ABC, order.* (Write the alphabet on the board for students to refer to.) *That means that a word beginning with* a *would be found before a word beginning with* m. (Point to *a* and then to *m* in the alphabet.) *If I alphabetized the words in this list, the list would look like this:*
   carriage
   gentle
   modern
   sly
   wealth

I know that I would find carriage *in the dictionary before the other words on the list.* (Highlight the first letter in each word and point to where that letter appears in the alphabet.)

Write these words on the board.
   sly
   safety
   soldier
   smock
   scent

Say: *Each of these words begins with* s. *They would all be found in the* s *section of the dictionary. How do I know whether to find* sly *before or after* scent? *I have to look at the second letter of each word. The second letter of* sly *is* l. *The second letter of* scent *is* c. (Point to where these letters appear in the alphabet.) *L comes after* c *in the alphabet, so* sly *comes after* scent. *I can alphabetize the list of words beginning with* s *by looking at the second letter of each word. The alphabetical order of the words would be*
   safety
   scent
   sly
   smock
   soldier

Display a dictionary page. Point out the guide words at the top of the page.

Say: *These are called guide words. They can help "guide" me to find words in the dictionary. The first guide word shows the word in the first entry on the page, and the second guide word shows the word in the last entry on the page.* (Point to the appropriate words.)

Write the following sets of guide words on the board.
   size—skate   sky—small   small—snore

Say: *The guide words tell me that every word on that page comes in alphabetical order between those two words. If I wanted to look up the entry for* sly, *I would look on the page with the guide words* sky—small. Sly *comes in alphabetical order between these two words.*

PART 2

On the board, write the word *candid* followed by its phonetic spelling: ˈkan-dəd.

Say: *One of the things a dictionary entry tells me is how to pronounce a word. Right after the entry word, the word is spelled the way it is pronounced. I can look at this spelling of* candid *and pronounce it correctly. If I am unsure of the symbols used to show the pronunciation, I can look at the pronunciation key at the bottom of the page.*

On the board, write *noun, verb, adjective,* and *adverb*. Remind students that a noun is the name of a person, place, or thing; a verb is an action word; an adjective describes a noun; and an adverb tells when, where, or how. Write the word *candid* on the board. Then write

v = verb	adj = adjective
n = noun	adv = adverb

Say: *One kind of useful information the dictionary gives is each word's part of speech. It tells whether a word is a noun, verb, adjective, adverb, or other part of speech. Suppose I want to use a word that is new to me,* candid. *I look the word up in a dictionary to find its meaning. The first clue to its meaning is its part of speech. The entry for* candid *is followed by its phonetic pronunciation. Then I see the abbreviation* adj. *This means that* candid *is an adjective. I cannot use the word as a noun or a verb. Then I look at the word's definition: "fair or honest." So I might use* candid *in a sentence like this: I gave an honest, candid answer. In this sentence,* candid *is an adjective. Each part of speech is abbreviated in a dictionary entry as shown on the board.*

COACH

Using **MatchWord**, create a worksheet of words for students to alphabetize. Include some words that have the same first letter but different second letters.

Say: *We can alphabetize many of these words by looking at their first letters. But some of the words begin with the same letter. So we must look at the second letter and see which comes first in the alphabet. Let's write the list of words in alphabetical order.*

When the list is complete, ask volunteers to explain how they alphabetized words with the same first letter.

Say: *Let's look up some words on the list in the dictionary. After we have found each word, we'll write the guide words that appear at the top of the page. Then we'll write the abbreviation for the word's part of speech. Finally, we can read the word's definition and use it in a sentence of our own.*

APPLY

Use **MatchWord** to create word lists. Have students use the lists for alphabetizing and for finding guide words, parts of speech, and definitions in the dictionary. The Activities Bank that follows provides ideas for helping students practice looking words up in a dictionary. You may want to pair ELL students with English Only students.

ASSESS

- Observe students as they complete the activities.
- Listen to students as they explain to the class how they alphabetize words with the same first letter and how they locate a word's part of speech in a dictionary entry.
- Use the assessment blackline master provided at the end of the unit to evaluate students' mastery of dictionary skills.

RETEACH

- Use **MatchWord** to create more lists of words for students to alphabetize and to find guide words and parts of speech for.
- Ask students to write the names of ten students in the class. Have them alphabetize the students' first names and then their last names.
- Have students write a list of five words that name a kind of flower, tree, or animal. Ask them to exchange lists with a partner and find the guide words in the dictionary for each word on the list.

ACTIVITIES BANK

We're on the Same Page

Divide the class into small groups. Using **MATCHWORD**, make word cards so that members of each group have different words beginning with the same letter. On the board, write possible guide words for each word card word. Have students decide which guide words their word comes between and write it on the board under the guide words.

Alphabetize Lists

Ask each student to look through a classroom book to find and write eight words that reflect the content of the book. Have students trade lists with a partner, put the words into alphabetical order, and find the dictionary guide words for each word. To extend the activity, have students write each word's part of speech.

Guess the Word

Have students work in pairs. Give each pair a dictionary. Have one partner select a word and give clues to help the other partner guess the word. Suggest that students use the guide words as one clue and the definition or part of speech as another. For example, *This word means a "small wagon." It is on the page with the guide words* carry—catch. (cart) Students can take turns guessing words.

Third and Fourth Letter Alphabetizing

To challenge students, use **MATCHWORD** to create lists of words with the same initial two or three letters, such as *mountain, more, most, move, morning, mother.* Have students put the words into alphabetical order and then explain how they did so. You can also have students make up their own lists of words with the same initial letters and give them to a partner to alphabetize.

Definition Challenge

Have each student find a challenging word in a textbook or other book in the classroom. Ask students to exchange words with a partner. Partners should look the word up in a dictionary and write a sentence of their own using the word. Then partners can exchange sentences and check for correct usage. The activity can be repeated several times.

Pronounce It Right

Use **MATCHWORD** to generate a list of words that may be challenging to pronounce. Have students look each word up in a dictionary and write its phonetic spelling. Then have groups of students take turns pronouncing the words. Possible words are *crevice, fragile, pseudonym, subtle,* and *transcend.*

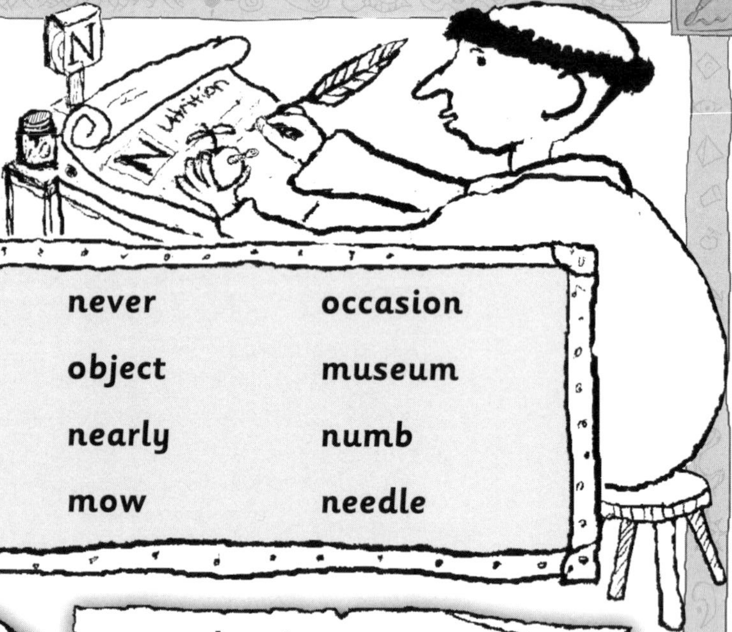

Write the words in the box
under the correct dictionary
guide words.

mutter	nutrition	never	occasion
oak	new	object	museum
nutmeg	nurse	nearly	numb
oatmeal	muddle	mow	needle

movie—myth

_____

_____

_____

natural—niece

_____

_____

_____

normal—nylon

_____

_____

_____

nylon—odd

_____

_____

_____

Context Clues

CONTEXT CLUES

BACKGROUND INFORMATION

In their reading, students often encounter unfamiliar words. They should learn to use surrounding words, or context, to find clues to any new word's meaning. Students need to understand that the immediate sentence may not provide enough clues; they may need to look at other samples of the passage. It is also wise to approach a new word from the inside. That is, readers can analyze the word to see if it contains familiar parts or if they have any prior knowledge of the word. Other strategies include deciding the word's part of speech and the class of things to which it belongs, then searching the context for examples and descriptions. These types of analysis help readers put together a working definition for the new word.

OBJECTIVES

The student will learn to
• analyze context clues in a passage to determine the meaning of an unfamiliar word or a multiple-meaning word
• analyze parts of an unfamiliar word to see if any of those parts are familiar
• recognize various types of context clues, such as examples, descriptions, mood of a passage, comparisons, contrasts, or cause-and-effect relationships

PRE-CHECK

Write the following sentences on the board and read them aloud.
> Beef must be <u>ground</u> in order to make hamburger.
> My <u>ritual</u> for grilling hamburgers is to light the coals, put on my apron, and pour a glass of lemonade.

Ask students to give the meaning of *ground* as it is used in the first sentence and the meaning of *ritual* in the second sentence. Have them explain how they were able to figure out these meanings. Encourage students to explore the overall meaning of each sentence and clues within it as well as analyze word parts. Use the discussion to see what students know about using context clues.

ELL SUPPORT

Second language learners will benefit from a preview of the word in its context. For example, prior to reading a selection, write several sentences using the words that are unfamiliar to allow ELL students a chance to predict the meanings of the new words by using the context. Direct the students to look at surrounding words used in each sentence to find clues to the meaning of the unfamiliar word. Encourage ELL students to talk about all possible meanings of the word.

DEMONSTRATE

The Demonstrate section of the lesson is divided into two parts. Part 1 explores the methods for determining which meaning of a multiple-meaning word is intended in the context of a sentence. Part 2 discusses how to explore an unfamiliar word and the words that surround it in order to decide its meaning.

PART 1

Write this sentence on the board and underline the word *race*.

> Our laws say that we cannot treat people unfairly on account of their <u>race</u>, creed, or color.

Say: *I know that the word* race *has several meanings. It can mean "a contest of speed," "to run fast," or "a group of people with common ancestry."* (Write these definitions on the board.) *How can I tell what meaning* race *has in this sentence? I will look at the context, or the words surrounding it, for clues. First, I'll look at the general subject of the sentence: it is about laws and treatment of people.* (Circle *laws* and *treat people*.) *This topic points to the third definition. Next, I'll look at other details in the sentence.* Race *is grouped with* creed *and* color, *as though they are similar things. I know that a person's color may be determined by his or her race, or heritage. These details also point to the third definition. In this sentence,* race *means "a group of people with common ancestry."*

Talk about the need to consider the context, or subject matter and details, of a sentence to decide which meaning of a multiple-meaning word is used.

PART 2

Write this sentence on the board and read it aloud. Underline the word *telecast.*

> Stay tuned for a live <u>telecast</u> of the concert.

Say: *This sentence has a word I do not know:* telecast. *I will try out some strategies for deciding the meaning of the word. First, I will look at the word closely. I will try dividing it into parts and seeing if I recognize any of the parts.* (Write the word as *tele/cast* on the board.) *I recognize* tele-; *it is part of other words I know, like* telephone *and* television. (Write these words below *tele* and draw arrows to them.) *I think maybe* tele- *has something to do with long distance, since these two machines let us hear and see things that are far away. I have seen* -cast, *too. It can be a cover on a broken arm or leg, or the action of throwing out a line, or a group of people in a play.* Cast *can also be part of other words, like* broadcast. (Write *broadcast* below *cast* and draw an arrow from *cast* to the second part of the word.) *These clues help me, but now I will look at the rest of the sentence for more clues. The phrase* stay tuned *and the word* live *are both used by television announcers. Putting these clues together, I can guess that a* telecast *is a program shown on television. Maybe it was made by putting together parts of the words* television *and* broadcast.

Talk about the importance of analyzing unfamiliar words while reading:
1. Look inside the word for parts I know and can define.
2. Look outside the word for clues to the overall meaning of the word in this context.

COACH

Using **MATCHWORD**, create a worksheet with sentences using multiple-meaning words students likely have seen, such as *angle, beam, cell, character, gear, occupy, overlook, report,* and *tear.* Below each sentence, list several meanings for the target word. If you have taught Part 2, you might make a second worksheet with sentences using words students are not likely to know. Underline the target word in each. Examples include *cleanser, delicate, dromedary, elegant, flammable, gawky, hot-headed, initial,* *magpie,* and *studious.* Leave space after each sentence as well as a write-on line. Provide opportunities for students to work with different types of context clues, including

- example: *The <u>bivalves</u>, which have two shells joined by a hinge, include clams and oysters.*
- description: *The <u>shield cone</u>, with its gentle slope and broad base, is the shortest kind of volcano.*
- mood: *When the claw touched her, Paula let out a <u>blood-curdling</u> scream and ran from the haunted house.*
- comparison: *Jim is <u>taciturn</u>; his father also says very little.*

Say: *Let's read the first sentence on the worksheet.* (for example, *Mom had a wide <u>beam</u> on her face when she heard the good news.*) *Now let's look at the meaning choices. Which meaning does the word have in this sentence? Let's think about the overall meaning of the sentence. It suggests that someone would be happy. How do we know that?* (There is good news and the beam is on Mom's face.) *Which meaning fits the context of being happy? Let's try substituting that meaning in the sentence: Mom had a radiant, happy look on her face when she heard the good news. Yes, that meaning makes sense, doesn't it? Let's mark that one.*

Continue with the other sentences on the worksheet, helping students analyze the sentence context to determine which meaning of each multiple-meaning word applies. On the second worksheet, help students first analyze the underlined word for word-part and structure clues, then look at the overall sentence for context clues to meaning.

APPLY

Use **MATCHWORD** to create activities that require students to use context to determine word meaning or that lead them to discuss the kinds of meaning clues they get from context. For example, you might make mini sentence strips, draw and write pages, and cloze sentence worksheets. The Activities Bank that follows provides ideas for helping students practice using context clues to decide meaning.

ASSESS

- Observe students as they complete the activities. Note in particular whether they can analyze words for familiar parts and get meaning clues from surrounding words.
- Point to words used in context on **MATCHWORD** blackline masters. Ask students to explain how they decided the meaning of each word.
- Use the assessment blackline master provided at the end of the unit to evaluate students' understanding of context clues.

RETEACH

- During reading, model with students how you analyze context to determine the meaning of an unfamiliar word. Point out different kinds of clues, such as examples, classes, descriptions, contrasts, and cause-and-effect relationships, in surrounding sentences.
- List simple multiple-meaning words (such as *ball, box, down, ear,* and *out*), and use them in context to give students practice at determining which meaning is intended. Gradually add harder words (such as *draw, flag, fork, lumber, major,* and *quarter*).
- Assign each student a new content-area word to learn. He or she is responsible for providing context clues (in sentences, in pantomimes, and in illustrations) to help others learn the word's meaning.

ACTIVITIES BANK

Context Webs

Select words unfamiliar to students. In the center of a sheet of paper, write a sentence rich in context clues for each word. Give each student a page. Ask students to highlight clues in the sentence, write what each clue told them about the word in circles around the sentence, and connect the circles to the clues with lines.

Context Riddles

Choose multiple-meaning words from students' reading materials. Copy the sentence(s), including context clues to the word's meaning, onto an index card. Have each student draw a card and make up a riddle for the word. Suggest that students use the sentence context clues and another meaning of the word in their riddle. For example, Sentence: *The prisoner lived in a windowless cell, just 6 feet by 6 feet.* Clues: *I am a room. I hold people inside to punish them. I am small and dark. I can also mean the smallest living thing. What am I?*

Guess the Animal

Play a game using multiple-meaning words that name animals: *bat, bear, cow, duck, fly, fish, flounder, swallow, worm,* and so on. Write each word on an index card; on the opposite side, write other meanings for the word. A player draws a card and writes a sentence for each meaning, leaving a blank where the word belongs. The player reads the sentences aloud. The first player to identify the animal wins a point. As an alternative, play Guess the Body Part, using words such as *arm, chest, ear, eye, face, foot, gum, hand,* and *teeth.*

"Meaning-ful" Scenes

Select verbs and adjectives that students do not know, such as *promenade* and *delectable.* Write a word on the board, then use it in a sentence. Have students act out the sentence to show the meaning of the word. Then write the sentence on the board and have students point out clues that told them the word's meaning.

Cloze Clues

On one side of the board, list these words: *distress, livable, magpie, felines, house-break, initial.* On the other side, write the sentences below. Divide students into teams and have each team decide which words belong in which sentences, using context clues. Ask each team to complete one sentence and to use colored chalk to circle clues that helped them. Have the team explain what the word means.

The ___ flight failed, but the second and third tries were successful.
The baby cried and kicked its feet to show its ___.
Of all the ___, the lion is my favorite.
The apartment had so much dirt and garbage that it did not appear ___.
The ___ perched on a branch and chattered noisily, looking like a gossip in a tuxedo.
We'd like to ___ the kitten, but so far she won't use the litterbox.

Name: _____

Date: _____

Read each sentence. Underline any clues about what the underlined word means. Write the word's meaning on the line.

That marshmallow is searing! It burns my mouth.

Keep all <u>flammable</u> materials away from flames and hot things.

_____

Herds of wild <u>bison</u> once roamed the plains; today, ranchers raise them like cattle.

_____

Scrooge is my favorite <u>character</u> in the story *A Christmas Carol*.

_____

Your beating heart acts like a pump to keep the blood <u>circulating</u> around the body.

_____

The hungry campers began to <u>devour</u> their bread and cheese quickly and silently.

_____

The whole room looked <u>festive</u> once we had put up balloons and streamers.

_____

I warned Ruby about the need for <u>secrecy</u>, but she blabbed to everyone about our plans.

_____

SECTION 8

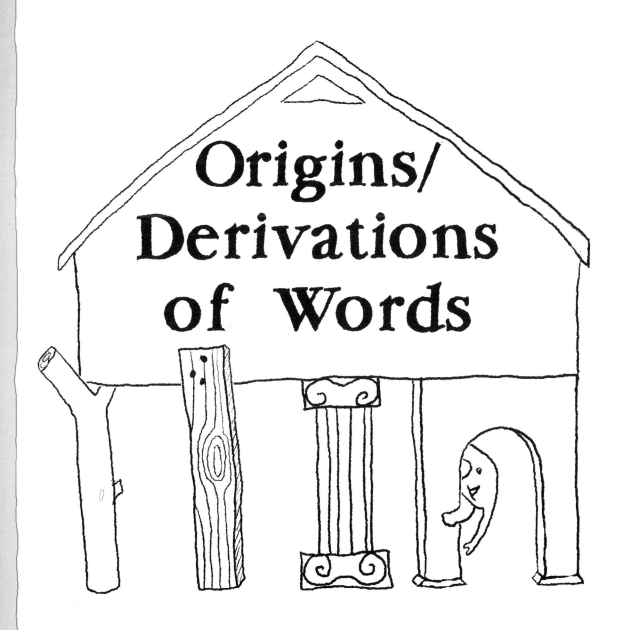

Origins/
Derivations
of Words

ORIGINS AND DERIVATIONS

BACKGROUND INFORMATION

The English language is a great borrower of words from other languages. Most of them came into English hundreds of years ago. (For example, many of our words originally came from Greek and Latin. These words were borrowed by European countries. They entered American English when people of those nationalities came to the United States to live.) Other words were added more recently (as a result of trade and contact with the cultures of many lands). Students need to understand that some of these words simply must be learned. However, learning the meanings, for example, of Greek and Latin roots, which appear in many English words, can be a helpful tool for students. If they learn to recognize roots such as *phon* (sound) and *scrib* (write), they can analyze and decode a number of words *(telephone, microphone, phonics; scribble, inscribed, script).*

OBJECTIVES

The student will learn to
- identify meanings of selected Greek and Latin roots
- analyze words to recognize Greek and Latin roots
- use words from other languages accurately in context

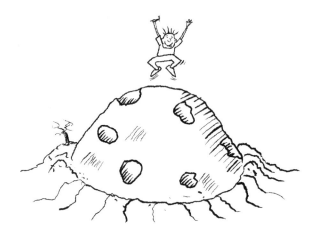

PRE-CHECK

Write the following sentence on the board, underline the words shown, and read the sentence aloud.

The <u>geologist</u> studied the <u>asteroid</u> that had fallen to Earth.

Ask students to tell the meanings of the underlined words and list any other words they know that share the same base, or root. Students' responses will help you assess their familiarity with Greek and Latin roots and the structural analysis of words.

ELL SUPPORT

Second language learners from a Greek or Latin language base will most likely connect to meanings selected from their given language background. For example, Spanish speakers will be able to connect to the Latin roots. Of note, English learners often have more difficulty in learning more basic academic words than words of Greek or Latin derivation.

DEMONSTRATE

The Demonstrate section of the lesson is divided into two parts. Part 1 discusses the meanings of common Greek and Latin roots. Part 2 focuses on identifying these Greek and Latin roots in unfamiliar words. You may wish to complete Part 1, then go on to the Coach section, coming back to Part 2 at a later time.

PART 1

Write this table on the board.

COMMON GREEK AND LATIN ROOTS

Root	Meaning	Origin	Example
aud	hear	Latin	auditorium
astro	star	Greek	astronaut
bio	life	Greek	biography
geo	earth	Greek	geography
ped	foot	Latin	pedal
phon	sound	Greek	microphone
port	carry	Latin	transport
scrib, script	write	Latin	scribble

Say: *This table tells me about Latin and Greek roots. The first column names roots, and the second column tells me their meanings; for example,* geo *means "earth." The third column tells which language the root came from—*geo *is Greek. The last column gives an example word in English that is built from the root. I can see that* geography *is derived, or made, using this Greek root because the letters* geo *appear in the word. I also know that* geography *is a subject in which we study the features of the Earth. It makes sense to learn that* geo *means Earth.*

Continue analyzing the roots in the table, noting the spelling and meaning of each root and relating it to a familiar word.

PART 2

Write this sentence on the board and read it aloud. Underline the word *inscribed.*

The names of heroes are <u>inscribed</u> on the memorial.

Say: *I don't know the word* inscribed. *First, I will look at the word and see if I can break it into parts. I see* -ed *at the end. This is an ending I can remove. I know* -ed *is added to verbs to make them past tense, so I know this word is an action word. The word begins with* in-. *I know this is a prefix, so I can remove it, too. What is left? The letters* scrib. *I remember from the table of Latin and Greek roots that* scrib *means "write."* Inscribed *might mean* wrote. *Now I'll look at the sentence to see if it gives me any clues to the meaning of* inscribed. *This verb describes an action about the names of heroes on a memorial. A memorial is usually a stone structure. Often, names or dates are carved into the stone. I think* inscribed *means "written or engraved."*

Continue analyzing words that have the Latin and Greek roots shown in the table in Part 1, for example, *biology, pedestrian, geode, inaudible,* and *deported.*

COACH

Using **MATCHWORD**, create a worksheet that lists Greek and Latin roots and their meanings and then gives sentences using words that contain those roots. Underline those words and provide a blank line after each sentence. Read each sentence with students. Ask them how they would find the meaning of the underlined word. Have them write the word's definition on the blank line.

Say: *How can we learn the meanings of the underlined words in these sentences? We can look for a Greek or Latin root and find the meaning of the root. We can also look at the whole sentence and think about what meaning fits this sentence. Let's look at the first sentence and underlined word.* (for example, *That centipede scurrying around in the tub scared me.) What root do we see in* centipede? *That's right. It has the root* ped. *Let's look at the chart to see what it means. It means "foot." Now let's look at the whole sentence. What does the sentence describe? How do the words* scurrying *and* scared *give us clues about the meaning of* centipede?

Continue with the other sentences on the worksheet.

APPLY

Use **MATCHWORD** to create activities that require students to use context and their knowledge of Greek and Latin roots to determine word meaning. These might include cloze sentences, crossword puzzles, word cards, and word sort columns. The Activities Bank that follows provides ideas for helping students practice identifying Greek and Latin roots in new words and determine the meanings of the words.

ASSESS

- Observe students as they complete the activities. Note in particular whether they can break difficult words into parts and locate roots and then use context to assist in determining logical meaning.
- Write the following words on the board near the table of Latin and Greek roots: *scribble, peddler, import, audible, biographer, microphone, astronomy, geometry.* Have students underline the Greek or Latin root they find in each word and predict the word's meaning.
- Use the assessment blackline master provided at the end of the unit to evaluate students' understanding of Greek and Latin origins of words.

RETEACH

- During reading, model with students how to identify roots in words and then use context clues to help determine the meaning.
- List one Greek or Latin root on the board, with its meaning. Write several words that are built from this root. Say each word and have students underline the root. Use the word in a sentence and have students tell its modern meaning and how they think the original Greek or Latin meaning fits.
- Assign each student a word with a Greek or Latin root to learn. He or she is responsible for teaching a small group the meaning of the root and several example words that use it.
- Have ELL students look through magazines and cut out words with a Latin or Greek origin. They may discuss the meanings with a partner and write sentences using the words.

ACTIVITIES BANK

Partner Practice with Word Cards

Write each Greek and Latin root on an index card. On the back, write the meaning of the root and an example word. Have partners use the cards as flash cards to learn the roots. As an alternative, students might play a game by drawing a card the partner cannot see and giving clues such as *This root means "carry." It is found in the word* transport. The player gets a point for each root he or she can name and spell.

Greek and Latin Root Crossword

Use **MATCHWORD** to create a crossword puzzle. As clues, give sentences with blanks and letters of the word that uses the root. For example, *1 down: An old ___dler carried goods for sale to the settlers.* (Answer: *ped*)

Glossary of Words from Latin and Greek

Divide students into small groups or pairs and give each group one of the roots from the table. Their job is to find as many words as possible that use this root, to write definitions for them, and to add an illustration showing how the root is related to the word. For example, *pedal* might feature a drawing of a foot on a bicycle pedal. Combine students' word pages into a classroom glossary.

Context Corner

Choose words with Greek or Latin roots from students' reading materials. Copy the sentence(s), including context clues to the word's meaning, onto an index card. Have each student draw a card and decide the meaning of the underlined word. The student then teaches this new word to another student by showing how to break it into parts, identify the root, and use the context clues in the sentence.

Word Contests

Divide students into small groups. Provide each group with a dictionary and a copy of the table of common Latin and Greek roots. Have the groups brainstorm a list of as many words as they can that use each root. Students are to write each word and its meaning on an index card and underline the root. Help groups add their words and meanings to a bulletin board list, with separate sections for each root. Challenge students to rearrange the words in each section to keep them in alphabetical order.

Words from Other Languages

	French	Spanish	American Indian
Easy	battle	alfalfa	chipmunk
	cent	alligator	maize
	court	cocoa	moccasin
	fashion	coyote	moose
	jean(s)	guitar	skunk
	prince/princess	rodeo	squash
	question	taco	woodchuck
	shock		
	French	**Spanish**	**American Indian**
Medium	ballet	cafeteria	avocado
	bureau	cannibal	chocolate
	denim	canyon	hammock
	jail	cockroach	opossum
	noble	lasso	potato
	saint	ranch	tomato
	soldier	mosquito	wigwam
	French	**Spanish**	**American Indian**
Hard	artillery	adobe	kayak
	caribou	armada	papoose
	cavalry	bravado	terrapin
	champagne	desperado	toboggan
	chic	enchilada	tomahawk
	defendant	tortilla	
	garage	tornado	
	quiche		

Read each sentence. Look at the underlined word. Look at the roots in the chart. On the line, write the root that is used to make the underlined word.

Root	Meaning	Root	Meaning
aud	hear	astro	star
ped	foot	bio	life
port	carry	geo	earth
scrib, script	write	phon	sound

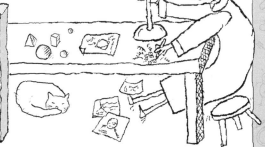

An <u>astronomer</u> needs a telescope. _____

The <u>symphony</u> will play a concert on Sunday. _____

I will <u>pedal</u> the bike up the hill. _____

Was there an <u>inscription</u> on the back of the locket? _____

The table is <u>portable</u> because it folds into a small size. _____

We studied the life cycle of frogs in <u>biology</u> class. _____

This kind of stone with crystals inside is called a <u>geode</u>. _____

Her voice was barely <u>audible</u> over the noisy fan. _____

Write the words that belong with each root on the line next to the root. Circle the root in each word.

audio	telephone	export	audience	pedal	geometry
portable	transporter	geography	peddler	phoneme	millipede

aud _____

geo _____

ped _____

phon _____

port _____

SECTION 9

Content-
Area Words

CONTENT-AREA WORDS

BACKGROUND INFORMATION

In their school careers, students will read many textbooks. Textbooks are often loaded with specialized vocabulary. These content-area words must be learned in order to master the concepts of the subject. Generally, textbooks are structured to help students learn vocabulary. A brief definition may be given when the term is introduced. The term may be set in bold type to call attention to it. Key terms may be defined in a glossary. In addition, the context will often be rich in clues that can provide understanding of the term. Students need to apply their ability to analyze context and word analysis to help them learn new vocabulary in the content areas. They will find that their ability to ask questions as they read and to understand organizational structures such as sequence and pattern are valuable when they encounter new vocabulary in textbooks. However, for these special and often technical terms, these skills will not always be enough. Students will also need to get in the habit of using the glossary and should review and use the terms in order to learn them well.

PRE-CHECK

Write the following sentence on the board and read it aloud. Underline *ecosystem* as you read these terms.

> An area in which living things interact with one another and their environment is known as an <u>ecosystem</u>.

Ask students to tell the meaning of the underlined word and to explain how they figured out its meaning. Students' discussion will help you assess their abilities to approach and understand new terms in content-area reading.

ELL SUPPORT

Second language learners will benefit from several instructional practices to build their understanding of specialized vocabulary. Direct and concrete experiences with content area words are recommended for ELL students. Where possible, support all lessons with visuals, structured discussion, and various grouping configurations such as working with a partner or in a small group.

OBJECTIVES

The student will learn to
- identify key content-area words and find out their meanings
- use a glossary to define specialized vocabulary
- use context and word analysis to predict the meanings of new content-area words

Demonstrate

The Demonstrate section of the lesson is divided into two parts. Part 1 explores strategies for finding definitions of terms in a textbook. Part 2 discusses how to use prior knowledge, context, and the nature of the topic in order to decide the meaning of an unknown word.

Part 1

Write this sentence on the board and underline the word *amphibians*.

> The frog, one of the most common **amphibians,** begins its life in water.

Say: *I am not sure what the word* amphibians *means. I see that it is set in bold type. This tells me it is a key word that I should learn. Usually, these key words are defined in the textbook's glossary, which is located at the back of the book. Sometimes they are defined on the side or at the bottom of the page on which they appear.*

Write this glossary entry on the board and read it aloud, underlining words as shown:

> **amphibian** (am ˈfi bē ən): a cold-blooded <u>vertebrate</u> that has a moist <u>skin</u> with no scales and lives part of its life <u>in water</u> and part <u>on land</u>.

Say: *Here is the glossary definition for* amphibian. *It tells me the larger group to which this animal belongs—the vertebrates. I can look up* vertebrates *if I need to, but I happen to know that this word means "animals with backbones." The glossary definition also gives me many details about the animal: it has skin that has to stay wet*

and it has no scales. Therefore, it makes sense that it lives part of the time in water. Now I can return to the lesson and reread the sentence in which the word occurs. (Reread the sentence above.) *I can picture what a frog looks like. I have seen a frog leaping into water. This helps me understand that amphibians have smooth, moist skin and adapt themselves to two environments: land and water.*

Part 2

Write this paragraph on the board and read it aloud, underlining words as shown.

> An organism's adaptations help it to survive in its <u>habitat</u>, or living place. One interesting adaptation is <u>camouflage</u>. The walking stick looks like a twig of the plant on which it lives. The fawn has a spotted coat that blends in with the dark and light of the brush where it is hiding.

Say: *This passage has two words I need to learn. I can look at the words around them to see if they give clues to the words' meanings. The phrase after* habitat *is "or living place." The author has put a simple definition into the sentence right beside the word. Now I'll look at* camouflage. *The sentence tells me it is one example of an adaptation. The first sentence told me that adaptations are ways a living thing has of surviving in its home. These facts let me know that* camouflage *is one way a plant or animal helps itself to stay alive and fit into its home. Now I'll look at the rest of the paragraph to see if it has more clues. The next two sentences give me two examples of animals that use camouflage. These examples show me that camouflage can be a body shape or a color pattern that helps an animal hide or blend in. Using all this information, I'll make up my own definition:* Camouflage *is an adaptation, such as a body shape or color pattern, that helps an animal fool its enemies by letting it hide or blend in with its surroundings.*

COACH

Using **MATCHWORD**, create a worksheet with short passages using science words, such as *community, deforestation, gene, habitat, niche, mammal, producers,* and *mammal.* Provide context clues, such as examples, synonyms, or definitions, for each word. Below each sentence, list several possible meanings for the target word.

Say: *Let's read the first sentence.* (for example, *The cutting of vast stretches of rain forest has forced us to consider the problems we will have because of <u>deforestation</u>.*) *What is the topic of this sentence? It talks about problems caused by cutting down the rain forests. What can we find inside the word* deforestation? *What ideas do you have about the meaning of the word? The sentence also tells us that vast, or huge, areas of forest have been cut down. How does this information affect your understanding of the word* deforestation?

Continue with the other sentences on the worksheet, having students analyze the sentence context to determine which meaning of each content-area word is most logical.

APPLY

Use **MATCHWORD** to create activities that require students to use glossary entries or context to determine meanings of content-area words and that call on students to study and learn the meanings of core content words. For example, you might make mini-sentence strips, word sorts, crossword puzzles, draw and write pages, and cloze sentence worksheets. The Activities Bank that follows provides ideas for helping students practice learning the meanings of content-area words.

Deforestation

ASSESS

- Observe students as they complete the activities. Note in particular whether they can locate and analyze context clues and overall topic to define new terms.
- Point to content-area words used in context on the **MATCHWORD** blackline masters. Ask students to explain how they decided the meaning of each word.
- Use the assessment blackline master provided at the end of the unit to evaluate students' understanding of content-area words and glossary functions.

RETEACH

- During reading, model for students how you check for definitions in a glossary or on the page where a term is introduced. Also, model how you analyze context to enrich the meaning of content vocabulary. Point out context clues, such as examples, descriptions, or comparisons, in surrounding sentences.
- List core terms in a content-area subject students are studying this week. Have them work in small groups or with a partner to locate the words in their texts and use pictures, context, and the glossary to learn the meaning of each word.
- Assign each student a new content-area word to learn. He or she is responsible for providing context clues (in sentences, in pantomimes, and in illustrations) to help others learn the word's meaning.

ACTIVITIES BANK

Context Webs

Select content-area words that students need to learn for current units of study. Write a two- or three-sentence passage rich in context clues for each word, positioned in the center of a sheet of paper. Give each student one page. Students are to highlight clues in the passage. Ask them to write what each clue told them about the word in circles around the sentence and connect the explanations to the clues with lines.

Strategies for Vocabulary Power

Write on the board a list of science vocabulary words for a specific unit, such as these: *rock cycle, water cycle, precipitation, erosion.* Make three hats of different colors, one for each of these strategies for learning meaning: **Red**—Break the word into parts and look for what you know about. **Blue**—Look at the context of the sentence and the general topic. **Yellow**—Discover the category or group (Ask *What is it?*), the description (Ask *What is it like?*), and any examples from the passage. Duplicate a text passage in which each of the science words appears, and distribute copies to students. Suggest a color of hat for students to put on as they attack each word to learn its meaning. Then allow students to switch hats to try different methods of getting meaning.

Glossary Champs

Divide students into teams. Provide each student with a glossary for a subject students are currently studying. Use **MATCHWORD** to make vocabulary word cards. Show a word card to the teams and say a sentence using the word in context. Have teams look up the word and read its definition as quickly as possible. Time how quickly they can find the answer. Challenge students to improve their speed at locating words in the glossary.

Subject Crosswords

Using **MATCHWORD**, create a crossword puzzle using vocabulary words from a math, social studies, or science unit students are studying. As clues, provide context-rich sentences with blanks where the vocabulary words belong. If necessary, also provide a word bank that includes the answer words and some other vocabulary.

ACTIVITIES BANK

Subject Glossaries

On the board, list words students need to learn for a current unit of study. Pair students and have partners use textbooks, glossaries, encyclopedias, and other resources to learn the meaning of each word. For each term, partners are to prepare a glossary entry that gives the group, description, and examples of the term. Encourage partners to add illustrations and example sentences to clarify meaning. Have students combine their entries into a mini-glossary.

Vocabulary Baseball

Choose core vocabulary terms students have learned in various subjects this year. Divide students into two teams. Each player gets an "at bat" by listening as you read a sentence using a vocabulary term and write the term on the board. An accurate definition gives a base hit to the player. In the first inning, use simple terms. Increase the level of difficulty as you proceed to additional innings.

Context Cards

Choose new content-area words you want students to learn. On one side of an index card, write a context-clue-rich sentence with a blank where the term belongs. On the other side, write the word. Pair students and give each pair one index card, sentence side up. Have them read the sentence and fill in the blank with a word or phrase that makes sense. Partners then turn over the card and read the word. Have them check the meaning in a dictionary or glossary. Then have them write a new sentence using the term in context.

WORD LIST

Content-Area Words

	Social Studies	Math	Science
Easy	capital citizen community crops families justice liberty police officer population president wealth	add bar graph circle congruent figures fact family fraction greater than/less than meter rectangle subtract sum (difference) triangle	atom equator erosion force glacier mammal mass muscle orbit tundra rock cycle wave
	Social Studies	**Math**	**Science**
Medium	agriculture campaign civilization climate continent custom desert economy mayor plateau prairie reign vessel	area array cylinder decimal diameter divisor/dividend equation estimate perimeter place value polygon quotient radius volume	acid algae base combustion community friction gene habitat lever mineral precipitation producers solar system
	Social Studies	**Math**	**Science**
Hard	cathedral commodity commonwealth famine latitude legislation longitude navigate policy resource revolution sanction tropical	base billion height least common denominator mean (average) negative integers prime numbers quadrilateral trapezoid variable	amphibian camouflage cell theory deforestation diffusion ecosystem food web hypothesis innate behavior niche protein solution X rays

Circle the best strategy or strategies to use to figure out the underlined word's meaning. Write the meaning of the underlined word.

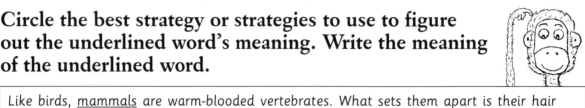

Like birds, <u>mammals</u> are warm-blooded vertebrates. What sets them apart is their hair and the milk-producing glands with which females feed their young.

Strategies: glossary   context   word analysis/previous knowledge

Definition: _____

Its poisonous skin gives the Poison Arrow frog a unique <u>niche</u> in the rain forest food web.

Strategies: glossary   context   word analysis/previous knowledge

Definition: _____

Two or more groups of different organisms live together and interact with each other, forming a <u>community</u>.

Strategies: glossary   context   word analysis/previous knowledge

Definition: _____

The <u>tundra</u> covers about one-tenth of the Earth's land surface, most of it above the Arctic Circle.

Strategies: glossary   context   word analysis/previous knowledge

Definition: _____

Early scientists studied plants and animals under the microscope. They saw that all these organisms seemed to be built of tiny similar units, or cells. Although they observed many types of cells, they noted that all cells were a basic, functioning living unit. These observations formed the nucleus of the <u>cell theory</u>.

Strategies: glossary   context   word analysis/previous knowledge

Definition: _____

SECTION 10

Figurative Language

FIGURATIVE LANGUAGE

BACKGROUND INFORMATION

Words that convey something beyond their literal meanings are called figurative language. Figurative language uses figures of speech to help readers picture what is happening, to create special effects, or to reveal surprising similarities between things. Three examples of figurative language are

- simile: a comparison using the word *like* or *as*—*His feet were as big as boats.*
- metaphor: a comparison stating that one thing is another—*Her voice is liquid velvet.*
- personification: a figure of speech giving human traits to nonliving things—*The wind sang a sad song.*

OBJECTIVES

The student will learn to
- distinguish figurative language from literal language
- identify similes, metaphors, and personifications
- tell what two things are compared in a metaphor or simile and name the object being personified
- explain the meanings of similes, metaphors, and personifications

PRE-CHECK

Write the following sentences on the board and read them aloud.

You are such an eager beaver.
This class is like a three-ring circus.

Ask students to explain what the first sentence is saying. Have them describe what they picture when they hear the sentence and tell what two things are being compared. Then have them tell what two things are being compared in the second sentence and what this comparison points out about the class. Use the discussion to see what students know about figures of speech such as metaphors and similes.

ELL SUPPORT

Second language learners will benefit from the opportunity to act out and talk about the different examples of figurative language. For ELL students with a limited degree of proficiency in English, the teacher should consider reading the examples aloud. ELL students may experience some difficulty in understanding the use of simile, metaphor, and personification, mostly due to their limited proficiency in English. Therefore, aural, oral, and visual supports will increase their opportunities for understanding.

DEMONSTRATE

The Demonstrate section of the lesson is divided into two parts. Part 1 teaches metaphors and similes; Part 2 teaches personification. Many students may be approaching figurative language for the first time. You may wish to teach Part 1, then move on to the Coach section of the lesson and come back to Part 2 on another day.

PART 1

Write this part of a poem on the board. Read it aloud as students follow along.

> The cow coming across the grass
> moves like a mountain toward us.

Say: *This part of a poem describes a cow walking toward some people. I see that it contains a comparison using the word* like. *This kind of comparison is called a* simile.

Circle the word *like* and label the example with the term *simile.* Underline the words *cow* and *mountain.*

Say: *The cow is compared to a mountain. I know that these two things are very different. For example, a cow is living and a mountain is not. The writer doesn't mean this comparison literally. Instead, she wants me to think about some ways the cow and mountain are alike. To a child, a cow looks huge, like a mountain. Parts of its shape might have angles like a mountain. This simile makes me look at the cow in a new way.*

Write this metaphor on the board and read it aloud.

> The road was a dusty ribbon wrapped around the hill.

Say: *This sentence also contains a comparison. It compares a road to a ribbon.* (Underline *road* and *ribbon.*) *It does not use the word* like *but instead says the road* was *a ribbon. I know that this kind of comparison is called a* metaphor. (Label the example with the term *metaphor.*) *I also know that the writer does not mean the road is literally a ribbon. However, he wants me to think about how they are alike. The road curves its way around the hill. A ribbon uncurling from a spool curves off into space. A ribbon wraps a package, and the road is fitted snugly against the hill, like a package. This comparison allows me to picture the scene it describes in a vivid way.*

PART 2

Write the following part of a poem on the board and read it aloud.

> Sun in the backyard grows lazy
> dozing on the porch steps all morning.

Say: *I see that in these lines, the sunlight is described as though it were living. It is lazy and dozes; these are human characteristics.*

Underline *sun, lazy*, and *dozing.* Draw a curved arrow from *lazy* and *dozing* back to *sun.*

Say: *Giving human qualities, feelings, or actions to nonliving things is called* personification. (Write the term *personification* above the example.) *I know that the writer does not really believe the sun is a person. This comparison gives me a way to relate the subject to myself. The sunlight is moving slowly and lying still on the rectangles of the porch steps. This is like a lazy person, who would move slowly and might well take a nap in the morning.*

COACH

Using **MATCHWORD**, create a worksheet that has sentences containing metaphors and similes and another with examples of personification. If you have covered both parts at the same time, you may wish to include all three figures of speech on one worksheet. Place a short line after each sentence and a long line below each sentence. Read each sentence with students. Have them identify the kind of figurative language used and then tell what things are being compared or what thing is being described as human. Have students write *metaphor, simile,* or *personification* on the short line and underline key words that show the comparison or human traits in the sentence. Discuss what the figurative language means and have students write a sentence explaining this on the line below the sentence.

Say: *Let's read the first sentence.* (for example, The boy's hair shone like a golden coin.) *What is the boy's hair compared to in this sentence? A simile uses the word* like *or* as; *a metaphor doesn't. Do you see the word* like *or* as *in this sentence? Is this a simile or a metaphor? Why do you think the boy's hair is compared to the coin?*

Continue with the other sentences on the worksheet, having students identify the figure of speech, underline the key words, and explain what the language means.

APPLY

Use **MATCHWORD** to create games and activities that require students to identify metaphors, similes, and personifications and use context to explain what they mean. For example, you might make draw and write pages, word pages, cloze sentences, and mini sentence strips. The Activities Bank that follows provides ideas for helping students practice using figurative language.

ASSESS

- Observe students as they complete the activities. Note in particular whether they can identify types of figurative language and get meaning from them.
- Point to similes, metaphors, and personifications on the **MATCHWORD** blackline masters that students completed. Have them explain what each one means.
- Use the assessment blackline master provided at the end of the unit to evaluate students' understanding of figurative language.

RETEACH

- Point out examples of figurative language in students' reading material. Ask students to explain why the literal meaning of the words does not fit. Discuss the figurative meaning of the words.
- Read students a poem that has many similes, such as Langston Hughes's "Dream Deferred" or Eve Merriam's "Willow and Gingko." Show the poem on the overhead and have students highlight each simile and tell what things are being compared.
- List figures of speech on the board. Have students write sentences using them and exchange papers. Invite pairs to tell each other what they think these sentences mean.
- Use **MATCHWORD** to create sentences that use personification. For example: *The black water is dreaming of the moon.* Have students circle the word or words that show human characteristics and underline the thing being compared to a person.

ACTIVITIES BANK

Picturing Figures of Speech

Using **MATCHWORD**, create cards with common figures of speech, such as those below, written on one side. Have students choose two cards each and draw a picture on the opposite side that shows the literal meaning of these words. Stack the deck of cards with the pictures face up. Play a game in which players take the top card and use the picture to guess the figure of speech. They then turn the card over, read the figure of speech, and explain its figurative meaning.

> It's raining cats and dogs.
> The wind moaned and shrieked at the windows.
> The sun smiled on us.
> The cold gave me a frog in my throat.
> The wilderness called to him.
> My best friend is like a security blanket.

Figurative Language Favorites

Have students read through poems or bring in favorite poems to find examples of metaphors, similes, and personifications. Students can read their poems (or excerpts of longer poems) to classmates, who try to identify the figures of speech and explain them. Then have students copy their poems onto clean paper, highlight the figures of speech, and add illustrations that show how the figurative language adds to the mood or ideas of the poem.

Figurative Language Baseball

Divide the class into two teams. Set up a baseball diamond in an open area of the room. Read a metaphor, simile, or personification to the "batter." He or she can get to first base by identifying what kind of figure of speech it is; to second and third bases by naming the things that are compared; and to home plate by telling what the figure of speech means. If the player can give only the first answer, he or she stops at first base. If this answer is wrong, he or she is "out." Continue play for one team until it gets three outs. Play for five innings.

Build a Simile

Use **MATCHWORD** to create sentence strips with incomplete similes, such as the following:

> When I am tired, I am as ___ as ___.
> When I am hungry, I am like ___.
> When I am sleepy, I am as ___ as ___.
> When I am mad, I am like ___.

Fold the strips and place them in a box or hat. Have students draw a slip and complete the sentence to make up a simile. They can write their similes on a clean sheet of paper and add an illustration.

ACTIVITIES BANK

Be the Poet

Make a worksheet with short poems or excerpts from longer poems. Leave some metaphors, similes, and personifications incomplete by replacing certain words with blanks. Pair students to read each poem or excerpt and choose words to fill in the blanks. Have pairs read their completed poems to the class and tell why they chose these words. You may want to have students vote on their favorite version before you read the poet's original. Discuss why the poet chose these words and what the figures of speech mean.

Class Book of Personifications

Have students work with a partner or small group to read poems to each other and find examples of personification. Alternatively, you might assign teams poems that contain personifications. Their job is to choose two or three examples and copy each one onto a blank sheet of paper. They then cooperate to create a humorous illustration showing the object with human characteristics.

Personifying Nature

Use **MATCHWORD** to create a list of words naming something in nature (for example, *stars, sky, sea, stone, dawn, clouds*) and a second list naming a human action (for example, *tells, looks, reminds, thinks, listens, remembers, dances*). Have students choose a word from each column and use this subject and verb to build a sentence. The sentence may be on one subject or describe other subjects in nature. (For example, *The stone listens carefully to the chattering of the wind and trees.*) Have students continue choosing pairs of words and writing sentences, then combine their favorites into a poem. Point out to students that they may have to drop the *-s* on the end of some verbs.

Picture Captions

Ask ELL students to either draw pictures or cut pictures from magazines. Have them write sentences to accompany the pictures that demonstrate their understanding of similes, metaphors, and personification.

Name:	Date:

Read each sentence in the first column. Draw a line to connect the figure of speech to its meaning.

Figure of Speech	**Meaning**
After the contest Joan felt like a limp dishrag.	The dishes moved and rattled.
The hose was a green snake hiding in the grass.	He's not funny or fun; people aren't comfortable with him.
The girls are like two peas in a pod.	She was very tired.
Don't invite him; he's such a wet blanket.	Raindrops tapped the roof again and again.
The tulips bowed their heads in the spring rain.	The lighthouse light was a steady beam you could see in the dark.
As the earth shook, the china danced on the shelves.	The long, thin hose lay in the deep grass.
The fall leaves were a painter's palette against the sky.	The radiator made lots of noise as it heated the room.
The lighthouse shone like a star through the night.	Rain had knocked the tulips over.
The rain was a steady drumming on the tin roof.	Bright colored leaves stood out against the sky.
The radiator groaned and whistled like an old man snoring.	The girls are close and alike in every way.

Finish each sentence to make a simile or metaphor.

When I am sleepy, I am like _____.

As I walked by the growling dog, my heart was a _____.